1 MONTH OF
FREE
READING

at
www.ForgottenBooks.com

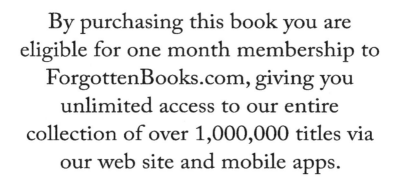

By purchasing this book you are eligible for one month membership to ForgottenBooks.com, giving you unlimited access to our entire collection of over 1,000,000 titles via our web site and mobile apps.

To claim your free month visit:
www.forgottenbooks.com/free999615

ISBN 978-0-260-99589-6
PIBN 10999615

This book is a reproduction of an important historical work. Forgotten Books uses
state-of-the-art technology to digitally reconstruct the work, preserving the original format
whilst repairing imperfections present in the aged copy. In rare cases, an imperfection in
the original, such as a blemish or missing page, may be replicated in our edition. We do,
however, repair the vast majority of imperfections successfully; any imperfections that
remain are intentionally left to preserve the state of such historical works.

Historic, archived document

Do not assume content reflects current
scientific knowledge, policies, or practices.

WHEAT SITUATION

WS-191   For Release March 6, A. M.   FEBRUARY 196

The price support loan is the principal factor establishing the level of wheat prices in the United States. The market price fluctuates around the loan as a result of general supply and demand considerations and seasonal factors. Over the past decade, the loan rate has been reduced substantially--from a high of $2.24 per bushel for the 1954 crop to $1.25 per bushel for the 1965 crop.

Cash receipts from wheat under the present program have been maintained at around $2.2 billion annually--about the same as that achieved under the mandatory program in effect until 1964. This has been accomplished by direct Government payments to farmers. These payments were made in the late 1950's under the Soil Bank Program and in more recent years under acreage diversion programs.

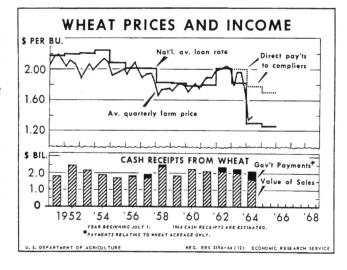

WHEAT PRICES AND INCOME

$ PER BU.

Nat'l. av. loan rate

Direct pay'ts to compliers

2.00

1.60

Av. quarterly farm price

1.20

$ BIL.

CASH RECEIPTS FROM WHEAT

Gov't Payments*

2.0

1.0

0

Value of Sales

1952 '54 '56 '58 '60 '62 '64 '66 '68

YEAR BEGINNING JULY 1.   1964 CASH RECEIPTS ARE ESTIMATED.
*PAYMENTS RELATING TO WHEAT ACREAGE ONLY.

U. S. DEPARTMENT OF AGRICULTURE   NEG. ERS 3394-64 (12)   ECONOMIC RESEARCH SERVICE

IN THIS ISSUE

Farm Price Remains Above Loan
U. S. Export Payments Increased
World Trade Declines
World Competition Increased

Published four times a year by
ECONOMIC RESEARCH SERVICE • U. S. DEPARTMENT OF AGRICULTURE

Table 1.- Wheat: Supply and distribution, United States,
average 1957-61, annual 1961-64

Item	Year beginning July				
	Average 1957-61	1961	1962	1963 1/	1964 1/ 2/
	Mil. bu.	Mil. bu.	Mil. bu.	Mil. bu.	Mil. bu.
Supply					
Carryover on July 1	1,162.0	1,411.2	1,321.9	1,194.9	901
Production	1,225.3	1,234.7	1,093.7	1,142.0	1,290
Imports 3/	8.0	5.9	5.5	4.3	4
Total	2,395.3	2,651.8	2,421.1	2,341.2	2,195
Domestic disappearance					
Food 4/	495.0	499.6	501.8	*533.0	480
Seed	62.0	56.0	60.6	62.8	70
Industry	.1	.1	.1	---	---
Feed 5/	45.9	54.3	21.4	*-15.3	65
Total	603.0	610.0	583.9	580.5	615
Exports 6/	547.7	719.9	642.3	859.5	**675
Total disappearance	1,150.7	1,329.9	1,226.2	1,440.0	1,290
Stocks on June 30	1,244.6	1,321.9	1,194.9	901.2	905

1/ Preliminary. 2/ Distribution items for 1964 are projected. 3/ Include full-duty wheat, wheat imported for feed, and dutiable flour and other products in terms of wheat. Exclude wheat imported for milling in bond and export as flour, also flour free for export. 4/ Includes shipments to U. S. Territories and wheat for military food use at home and abroad. 5/ This is the residual figure, after all other disappearance has been taken into account; assumed to roughly approximate wheat used for feed. 6/ Include flour wholly from U. S. wheat and other products in terms of wheat. Include exports for relief or charity by individuals and private agencies. Beginning in 1962-63, an allowance is made for donations of bulgar and rolled wheat which are not included in Census data. The wheat equivalent of these items is estimated for 1962-63, 3.6 million, and 1963-64, 7.8 million bushels.

* The quantity of wheat fed on farms where grown was estimated at 20 million bushels in the SRS publication, Field and Seed Crops--Production, Farm Use, Sales and Value, May 1964. Use of new-crop wheat, prior to June 30, was exceptionally heavy and resulted from the sharp reduction in the 1964 loan rate from that of 1963. Thus, supply and disappearance data are subject to more than usual discrepency. The food item is not the quantity consumed but the quantity processed for food. **May not be fully attained due to dock strike.

```
- -- ----- --------- -
```
THE WHEAT SITUATION
```
- -- ----- --------- -
```

Approved by the Outlook and Situation Board, February 26, 1965

CONTENTS

SUMMARY

The 1964 wheat crop, placed at 1,290 million bushels, is in balance with expected disappearance for 1964-65. As a result, the ending carryover on June 30, 1965, may be about the same as the 901-million-bushel carryover at the beginning of the current marketing year. The export estimate for 1964-65 remains at 675 million bushels, although it may not be fully attained as a result of the dock strike. In 1963-64, U. S. exports reached a record 860 million bushels as a result of a world-wide wheat shortage. The record world wheat crop and the intense competition among exporting countries in 1964-65 are primarily responsible for the reduced export estimate this year.

Based on the composition of exports during the July 1964-January 1965 period, commercial exports in 1964-65 are likely to represent the smallest proportion of total exports since World War II. Government-financed Food-for-Peace exports during the first 7 months made up an unusually large share of the total exports. India continued to be the major taker of U. S. wheat and received over 130 million bushels during July-January, all under the Food-for-Peace Program.

To maintain a competitive position in the world market for commercial exports, the United States reduced its export price by increasing export payment rates on wheat and flour in late January 1965. For example, the export price of hard red winter, the leading export wheat, was decreased as much as 19 cents per bushel.

Wheat prices remained high relative to the price support loan during July 1964-February 1965, the first 8 months of the current marketing year. Farm prices rose steadily during the first 6 months and declined only slightly in January and again in February. The season average price received by farmers for wheat in 1964-65 was estimated in December at $1.38 per bushel. When an allowance is made for the marketing certificate payments received by farmers participating in the 1964 Wheat Program, the adjusted season average price is about $1.69 per bushel.

Price support loan activity for the 1964 crop has been heavy. Withholding wheat from the market has been the major factor keeping prices above the loan. In turn, with high market prices, CCC sold large quantities of wheat at the statutory minimum sales price to meet the demands of the market.

World trade in wheat and flour during 1964-65 is expected to be sharply below the record 2.0 billion bushels that moved during 1963-64, but likely to be the third highest of record. The large 1964 crops in most exporting and importing countries have stimulated competition and world wheat prices have generally weakened. The condition of the 1965 world winter wheat crop points to another good harvest. Acreage planted to winter wheat in Western Europe has come through the winter in good condition. Prospects for wheat in Eastern Europe are uncertain. A normal winter wheat crop in the Soviet Union appears likely.

CURRENT SITUATION AND OUTLOOK

All Wheat

January 1 Stocks
Smallest Since 1958

Stocks of wheat held in all positions on January 1, 1965, totaled 1,442 million bushels, 11 percent below those of a year earlier and 25 percent below the 1959-63 average. Of the total, 1,052 million were held off farms with the remaining 390 million on farms (table 10).

About 63 percent, or 902 million bushels, of the January 1 stocks were owned or controlled by the Commodity Credit Corporation compared with 70 percent a year earlier. Of this, CCC owned 712 million bushels and 190 million were under loan--about 138 million bushels from the 1964 crop and 52 million bushels under reseal from earlier crops.

January 1 Stocks Indicate
Large Residual Feed Item

Total disappearance of wheat during July-December 1964, indicated by January 1 stocks, was 750 million bushels (table 21). This was somewhat

above the total disappearance of 725 million bushels in the year-earlier period
and substantially above the 1958-62 average of 587 million for that period.
Disappearance items that can be accounted for during July-December 1964 include
exports and shipments of wheat, flour and products at 396 million bushels, food
use of wheat at 242 million, and use of wheat for seed at 50 million. The data
on food use and exports are based on Bureau of Census reports. The quantity of
wheat used for seed was derived by applying a normal seeding rate to the acreage seeded to winter wheat in the fall of 1964, as reported by the USDA.

After all known disappearance in the July-December 1964 period has been
taken into account, the residual figure of 62 million bushels results and is
assumed to roughly approximate wheat used for feed. This derived feed use is
the largest in any half-year period since January-June 1956. See tables 21
and 22. However, these tables indicate that use of feed calculated as a residual is often erratic since it absorbs statistical errors and discrepancies
in data. For this reason, in some periods negative feed values appear, indi-
cating that the residual feed concept is not always meaningful and in many in-
stances is misleading.

October Feed Estimate Unchanged

The residual method indicates heavy feeding during the first half of
the 1964-65 year and this would be easy to understand in view of the price relationships between wheat and feed grains in many areas of the United States.
These price relationships, shown in table 12 for the first 2 quarters of 1964-
65, indicate that wheat has been an attractive feed item in the soft wheat areas
of the East and Pacific Northwest. This relationship, favorable to wheat feeding, generally continued in January and February. However, since there is no
statistically reliable information on the quantity of wheat fed in the first
half of the year or what may be fed during the second half, the earlier estimate of 65 million bushels for the 1964-65 year still stands.

Food Use of
  Wheat Unchanged

During July-December 1964, 290 million bushels of wheat were ground
for flour and approximately 50 million bushels of flour and products (wheat
equivalent) were exported (table 20). A larger quantity--305 million bushels--
was ground for flour during July-December 1963 with about 48 million bushels
(wheat equivalent) of this being exported during the period. The reduction in
domestic mill grind this year reflects the sharp cutback in milling during July-
August 1964, following the start of the certificate program on July 1. The
estimate of wheat used for food for the entire 1964-65 marketing year is continued at 480 million bushels (table 1). Wheat ground during June 1964, last
month of the 1963-64 marketing year, totaled 62 million bushels--the largest
monthly grind since March 1947 and about 15 million more than that ground in
June 1963. While the nature and timing of the 1964 wheat program caused millers
to alter their relative use of old- and new-crop wheat during the entire May-
September period, such action had no effect on calendar year 1964 totals, either

in the quantity of wheat used for food or total or per capita flour consumption (tables 19 and 20).

Exports Decline
During July-January

The earlier export estimate for 1964-65 of 675 million bushels is unchanged although it may not be fully attained as a result of the prolonged dock strike. Based on inspection data, exports of wheat as grain during the first 7 months of the current marketing year have declined from the same period a year earlier (table 3). Of the 367 million bushels inspected--about 33 million below a year earlier--only about 18 percent was shipped under commercial terms. In the same period a year earlier, commercial sales accounted for almost 40 percent of the wheat inspected for export.

Large wheat crops in many of the traditional exporting countries, as well as improved crops in importing countries, have sharply restricted U. S. commercial exports through January. Shipments under Government-financed programs, particularly P.L. 480, comprised about 82 percent of total exports during July-January. This is substantially above a year earlier and somewhat above the long-time annual average of about 70 percent. During the first 3 weeks in February, inspections totaled only 10 million bushels.

India continued to be the major taker of wheat from the United States, receiving about 133 million bushels during the July-January period. All of this wheat was moved under P.L. 480. Pakistan and Brazil were also recipients of large Food-for-Peace wheat shipments (table 5). Major commercial buyers this year include Japan, 28 million bushels, and The Netherlands, 6 million.

Exports of wheat flour during July 1964-January 1965, based on registrations for export payment, totaled 59 million bushels (wheat equivalent), slightly below a year earlier. The composition of flour exports, like that for wheat, is heavily weighted by those made under Government-financed programs (table 3). The United Arab Republic continued during this period to be the largest individual taker of flour with all of its purchases under P.L. 480.

Export Payment
Rates Increased

Maintenance of a high level of world wheat prices has encouraged increased wheat production in many countries. This price level primarily resulted from the United States and Canada withholding their surpluses from the market. Supply and disappearance of wheat in the major countries that compete with the United States in the world market are shown in table 28. The steady build-up in world wheat production and supplies has resulted in heavy sales by many of our major competitors during the current year at generally lower prices. The United States sharply increased its export payments for both wheat and flour, beginning January 25, 1965. This had the effect of lowering U. S. export prices to meet competition in world markets. U. S. export payment rates for wheat and flour are shown in table 24.

The lower export payment rates that had prevailed during the first half of the marketing year were the result of lower market prices in the United States and did not affect the net export price which was about the same as in earlier years. Prior to the January 25 increase, export payment rates under the current wheat program had been substantially below those required under earlier domestic wheat programs. The last line in table 24 provides the export payment rate for 1 day after the new payment rates were put into effect. While the present export payment rate is considerably larger than that in effect prior to the increase, it is still well below the payment rate of earlier years. It is generally felt that the new export payment rates will enable the United States to hold its own in the current world commercial market.

Carryover to Remain Stable

The supply of wheat in 1964-65 is now placed at 2,195 million bushels (table 1). This consists of the July 1, 1964, beginning carryover of 901 million bushels, the 1964 crop of 1,290 million, and imports estimated at 4 million. A supply of this size is below that' of recent years and is the smallest since 1957-58.

Domestic disappearance for 1964-65 is estimated at 615 million bushels (table 1). The quantity of wheat used for food in the United States continues to be estimated at 480 million bushels. The difference between this lower estimate of wheat used for food and the approximately 500 million bushels of many earlier years does not affect the quantity of wheat that actually will be consumed in the United States. Rather, it only affects the distribution of use by flour millers of the 1963 and 1964 crops (table 20). Wheat used for seed is placed at 70 million bushels and that estimated for feed use remains unchanged at 65 million, as previously explained. This domestic disappearance, together with exports of 675 million bushels, indicate a total disappearance of 1,290 million bushels. Since this disappearance is about the same as the production estimate, ending carryover on June 30, 1965, is expected to be around 905 million bushels, about unchanged from the beginning carryover on July 1, 1964.

Farm Prices
Continue Strong

The average price received by farmers for 1964-65 was estimated in December 1964 at $1.38 per bushel. This price is computed by weighting estimated season average State prices by estimated quantities sold and includes an allowance for unredeemed loans. Monthly prices received by farmers continued to run above support all during harvest and rose steadily each month through December when they averaged $1.39. In January 1965, the farm price of wheat declined 1 cent and in February it declined further. (table 9).

The national average loan rate for 1964-crop wheat has been established at $1.30 per bushel. Loan rates were raised by about 6 cents per bushel in the heavy-producing Southern Great Plains to reflect reductions made last fall in railroad freight rates. This had the effect of raising the national average loan rate to $1.32 per bushel.

"Adjusted" Season
Average Prices

Farmers participating in the 1964 Wheat Program received supplementary payments in the form of marketing certificates. The additional income from these certificates has not been included in the season average price received by farmers. A similar situation existed in 1963-64. Under the 1963 Wheat Program, a direct payment also had been made to farmers but it did not constitute as important a part of their income as did the 1964-crop payment. These basic changes in program concepts no longer make the price received by farmers an accurate or complete measure of farmers returns from wheat.

Table 16 considers the farmers' income based on their production valued at the season average price plus direct payments from the Government. Acreage diversion payments and Soil Bank payments are not included since these do not specifically relate to production. The season average price for wheat in 1963-64 was $1.85 but, with the price support payments of the 1963 Program included, the adjusted price is $1.92. With the inclusion of the marketing certificate payments in 1964-65, the adjusted season average price received by all farmers is raised from $1.38 per bushel to the blend price of $1.69. This represents an increase of 31 cents per bushel over the actual season average price compared with an increase of 7 cents in the adjusted season average price for 1963-64. The farmer participating in each of these Wheat Programs actually received a greater differential over the season average price than is indicated because these "adjusted" averages include all of the non-participants. An approximation of the "adjusted" price received by the farmer participating in the 1964 Program, based on the $1.38 season average price to all farmers and usual distribution of both certificates on normal production, would be about $1.80 per bushel.

CCC Activity Heavy

Farmers had placed about 188 million bushels of 1964-crop wheat under loan through January 31, 1965 (table 11). This was the last day that farmers could get approval on loan applications for 1964-crop wheat. They had until February 28 to decide on the total quantity they would actually put under loan. The February loan activity report will be available in mid-March. The total placed under the price support program through January 1965 was about 16 million bushels above that of a year earlier and the quantity outstanding under loan on this date was 43 million bushels above. The quantity remaining under reseal on January 31 was below that reported for January 31, 1964.

Sales and dispositions by CCC during July 1964-January 1965 totaled 225 million bushels, slightly smaller than those of the same period in 1963-64 (table 11). Sales at the statutory minimum—105 percent of the current loan rate plus carrying charges—for unrestricted use during July-January this marketing year were greater than those in the same period

a year ago with most of these sales made during the early part of the current
marketing year.   In contrast, the quantity of wheat delivered against Payment-
in-Kind (PIK) script was off sharply from the year-earlier level. The heavy
statutory minimum sales stemmed from the high level of market prices relative
to the loan whereas the decline in PIK dispositions was the result of the lower
export payments.

PIK Program
   Broadened

        PIK certificates earned on wheat exports are now redeemable in any CCC-
owned commodity offered for sale under a regulation issued or upon announcement
by CCC providing for redemption of such certificates. Tobacco under loan is
also available upon CCC announcement. Formerly, wheat certificates were re-
deemable only in wheat. The Payment-in-Kind program for wheat has been in
operation since September 1956. It covers all commercial and Title I, P.L.
480 (foreign currency sales) exports. Excluded from PIK are Title II, P.L.
480 (Government to Government donations), Title III, P.L. 480 (barter) and CCC
credit sales. Wheat for these programs comes from CCC stocks and is priced at
the world level.

        Up until late October 1964, all export payments for wheat flour were made
in cash regardless of the type of program. Since last October, the entire cost
of donation flour and bulgar for both domestic use and export has been paid for
in PIK certificates. Wheat redeemed with these certificates, as in the case
of the PIK wheat grain, must be exported. Based on the level of the flour and
bulgar donation programs in recent years, about 60 million bushels of wheat a
year could be supplied by CCC under this provision.

IWA Pact
   Extended

        The present International Wheat Agreement, scheduled to expire on July
31, 1965, was extended by the members for an additional year, subject to approval by their Governments. The 1-year extension was adopted on recommendation
of the United States. Most other members of the International Wheat Council
favored at least a 2-year extension. All provisions continue the same including
the maximum and minimum prices of $2.02½ and $1.62½, U. S. money, basis No. 1
Manitoba Northern wheat, in bulk in store, at the Lakehead. With the addition
of Rhodesia, the pact now includes 10 exporting and 39 importing countries.

"Free" Supply
   More than Adequate

        The "free" supply of wheat for the entire year, as estimated on January
31, was about 90 million bushels greater than the estimated total disappearance
of 1,290 million for 1964-65. The computed "free" supply is composed of the
July 1, 1964, carryover in private hands, estimated at 20 million bushels, the
1964 crop of 1,290 million and sales and dispositions by CCC during July-January

of 225 million. Imports are not included since they account for less than a million bushels. These items provided a total free supply of 1,535 million bushels, including the additions to the supply through January. However, about 156 million bushels of 1964-crop wheat were outstanding under price support loan on January 31, reducing the free supply, as of this date, to 1,379 million.

Through January 31, farmers had placed 187.5 million bushels of 1964-crop wheat under loan and had redeemed 31.4 million. Since the quantity of old-crop wheat under reseal loan on January 31, 1965, 51.7 million bushels, was about the same as that of July 1, 1964 it did not affect the free supply during July-January. Farmers had made applications for price support loans and purchases for 293 million bushels of 1964-crop wheat by January 31, the close of the loan application period. This was about 105 million bushels more than the 188 million they had actually put under loan by that date but they had through February 28 to carry out their application plans. This additional quantity could more than absorb the surplus "free" supply if it is put under loan and delivered to CCC. The loans mature on March 31. See table 15.

The figures and calculations are for all wheat and the free supply situation for the various classes could vary.

CURRENT SITUATION AND OUTLOOK

Wheat by Classes

Revised production figures, based on the December crop report, and changes in the distribution of the export estimate, due to shifts in emphasis on export programming, have changed the supply, disappearance and carryover estimates of several classes of wheat.

Hard and Soft Red Winter Wheats

The supply of hard red winter wheat is now placed at 1,310 million bushels. The estimate of exports of this class has been reduced to 460 million bushels from the earlier estimate of 490 million. During July-January this year 291 million bushels of this wheat were inspected for export compared with 234 million during the same period a year earlier (table 3). Less than 10 percent of the hard winter exports were made for dollars. Domestic disappearance has been raised slightly and carryover stocks on June 30, 1965, are now put at 582 million bushels (table 2).

The total supply of soft red winter wheat is placed at 233 million bushels. The ending carryover for the 1964-65 marketing year is now estimated at 20 million bushels, sharply below the earlier estimate of 45 million. The principal reason for the lower carryover is an increase of 30 million bushels in projected exports to a level of 70 million. Exports of soft red, grain only, totaled 32 million bushels during July-January with two-thirds moving under Government programs. Domestic disappearance of this wheat is placed slightly below the earlier estimated of 145 million bushels (table 2).

The price of No. 1 Hard winter, ordinary protein, at Kansas City rose from mid-October to late November. Since then it has declined but is still well above the loan (table 6). The price of No. 2 Red Winter at St. Louis has risen since mid-October; however, this rise has been erratic. The spread between soft red winter wheat prices and prices of hard winter wheat narrowed considerably in January (table 6).

Hard Spring and Durum Wheat

The total supply of hard red spring wheat for 1964-65 is now placed at 358 million bushels. Exports of this wheat during the current year are now estimated at 30 million bushels, a reduction of 10 million from the previous estimate. During July-January, only 7 million bushels were inspected for export but nearly all of this was sold for dollars. The carryover estimate for the end of the 1964-65 marketing year has been raised slightly to 198 million bushels (table 2).

The supply of durum wheat is estimated at 107 million bushels, an alltime record. Exports of durum continue to be carried at 5 million bushels for the current year, although during July-January they totaled only a million bushels. Domestic disappearance of this wheat is placed at 27 million bushels and a carryover of 75 million bushels is indicated for June 30, 1965.

The price of No. 1 Dark Northern Spring wheat, ordinary protein, at Minneapolis has risen steadily since mid-October. The price of hard spring wheat normally runs above the price of hard winter wheat and, in recent months, the price spread between these has generally widened (table 6).

White Wheat

The total supply of white wheat is currently estimated at 187 million bushels, about 150 million of this is in the West and the remainder is in the East--largely in New York and Michigan. The export estimate for all white wheat during 1964-65 has been raised slightly to 110 million bushels from the earlier estimate of 100 million (table 2). About 35 million bushels of white wheat were exported during July-January with half of this moving for dollars. As a result of the new export estimate, the carryover on June 30, 1965, is now estimated at 30 million bushels compared with the previous estimate of 41 million.

The price of No. 1 Soft White wheat at Portland rose steadily during late October and early November. Since then it has shown little fluctuation (table 6).

PROSPECTS FOR 1965-66

Winter Wheat
Seedings Large

The December 1964 seeding report indicated that farmers put 45.1 million acres in winter wheat for harvest in 1965. This is nearly 2 million acres more than was planted in December 1963 for harvest in 1964 and is the largest winter wheat seeding since the fall of 1952. Based on December 1 conditions, an acreage of this size would provide a 1965 winter wheat crop of 1,042 million bushels, somewhat above the 1964 crop.

Seeding in the important hard winter wheat States was sharply above that of a year earlier and the 1959-63 average (table 14). Kansas, the leading wheat State, reported an increase of 8 percent in acreage seeded. Oklahoma and Texas reported increases of 9 and 4 percent, respectively. Montana had a 28 percent increase, the largest of any state. Large increases in seeded acreage were also reported in the Pacific Northwest, where Washington indicated a 16 percent increase in acreage seeded.

In the major Eastern soft wheat States, the acreage seeded for harvest in 1965 was considerably below year-earlier levels. Ohio and Indiana reported decreases of 11 and 14 percent, respectively.

Under the 1965 Wheat and Feed Grain Programs, farmers having both a wheat acreage allotment and a feed grain base acreage may elect to substitute acreage if they are enrolled in both of these grain programs and adhere to the provisions of each. The pattern of winter wheat seeding of last fall reflects the desire of wheat farmers in the commercial wheat areas of the Southern Great Plains and the Pacific Northwest to produce wheat in place of barley, oats, rye, and to some extent, perhaps grain sorghum. The reductions in wheat seeding in the soft winter wheat areas of the East probably resulted from farmers' plans to substitute corn for wheat. The extent of possible shifts in acreages between grains cannot be fully appraised until the acreage diversion signup now underway is completed.

Spring Wheat Signup

The signup period for spring wheat and feed grains started on February 8 and continues until March 26. Through February 18, about 5.8 million acres of winter and spring wheat was enrolled in the program. About 4.0 million acres of this indicated acreage diversion represents the 10 percent reduction in allotments from the allotments in effect in 1963. The remaining 1.8 million acres is additional diversion from the 1965 allotment. Signup for the predominantly winter wheat areas took place last fall. Total indicated diversion for winter wheat was 5.5 million acres, of which 3.9 million represented the difference between the higher acreage allotment of 1963 and the present smaller allotment. Farmers who signed up in the winter wheat area, as well as those enrolled during the current signup, can change their enrollment intentions at any time prior to March 26.

Light Loss of Fall-
seeded Grains

Mild temperatures during January in the Southern Plains favored winter grains in areas where moisture was available. Growth was limited, but winter wheat was considered in good to excellent condition from central Kansas southward through Oklahoma into Texas. Snowfall late in January alleviated somewhat critical moisture-shortage areas stretching from the Panhandle areas of Texas and Oklahoma through eastern Colorado and western Kansas, but wheat will need more moisture before growth starts in the spring.

In Nebraska and South Dakota, the dry, windy weather was detrimental to winter wheat before snowcover fell on January 22. Moisture reserves are low and spring rains will be needed for good crop development. January conditions were generally favorable for wheat in the central Corn Belt and stands improved during the month.

Fall-seeded grains and winter pasture crops were in generally good condition in the Southeast. Grain fields in the Pacific Northwest were subjected to erosion and flooding from heavy rains in late January. This damage added to the losses from a December storm and extensive reseeding will be necessary in some areas.

Large 1965
Crop Likely

Based on the anticipated substitution of wheat for barley, oats, and rye, it is estimated that around 13 to 14 million acres of spring wheat may be planted. An acreage of this size would be somewhat larger than the 10 to 12 million acres of the last 5 years. With the average yield of recent years adjusted for trend, this acreage could produce a crop of about 300 million bushels. When added to the estimated winter wheat crop of 1,042 million bushels, a total wheat crop of about 1,345 million is indicated for 1965.

1965 Program Provisions

For the first time, substitution will be permitted between wheat and feed grain acreages in 1965 for farmers signing up for both programs. Price support loans are available to producers planting feed grains on wheat acreage, but this grain is not eligible for price support payments. Wheat planted on feed grain acreage also is eligible for loans, but not for domestic or export certificates. The national average price support loan rate for wheat is $1.25 per bushel, 5 cents less than for 1964. The domestic certificates will be 75 cents per bushel, 5 cents more than in 1964 and the export certificate will be 30 cents per bushel, also 5 cents higher. Wheat and feed grain loan rates and payments are shown in table 17.

A wheat producer, to be eligible for price support loans and domestic and export certificates, must participate in and comply with provisions of the 1965 Wheat Program. To obtain diversion payments, a producer may elect to diver an additional acreage of 10 to 20 percent of his farm allotment. In the case of farms with small allotments, enough more acreage may be diverted to make a total diversion of 15 acres, including the minimum for which no payment is made. Diversion payments earned are based on 50 percent of the county price support loan rate times the farm's normal yield per acre.

Substitution between feed grains and wheat will be permitted for farmers signing up to participate in both the wheat and feed grain programs. This substitution applies to wheat, corn, barley, and grain sorghums. Producers electing to use the wheat-feed grain substitution provisions and also requesting establishment of an oat-rye base for the farm are required to divert 20 percent of the oat-rye base to a conserving use. Payment for such diversion will be at a rate equal to 25 percent of the wheat diversion rate per acre for the farm. This would enable him to grow wheat on the oat-rye acreage plus growing wheat on all or a part of the permitted feed grain acreage. If this option is used, corn, barley, and grain sorghums cannot be produced on the oat-rye base, nor on the farm's wheat allotment.

Acreage diversion provisions of the 1965 Feed Grain Program are practically the same as those of the 1964 program. To be eligible for price support, a producer must divert at least 20 percent of his base acreage to soil-conserving uses. The maximum diversion is 50 percent of the base, or 25 acres, whichever is larger. If the diverted acreage is between 20 and 40 percent of the base, diversion payments will be the county support rate applied to 20 percent of the normal production for the first 20 percent diverted and 50 percent of the normal production on the remaining percentage. A producer diverting 40 percent or more of his base would receive a diversion payment based on 50 percent of normal production on all the diverted acreage.

The base acreage for corn, sorghums, and barley is determined from the 1959 and 1960 average adjusted acreage, the same as in the past 4 years. Normal production is based on the 1959-63 average yields and the farmer's base acreage. In 1964, normal production was based on 1959-62 yields. Since national yields have trended upward through 1963, this generally will increase the normal production for many feed grain producers.

Farmers taking part in 1965 Wheat and Feed Grain Programs again may substitute certain crops on land diverted from wheat and feed grain production. These crops are guar, sesame, safflower, sunflower, castor beans, and flaxseed, plus mustard seed on feed grain acreage. Plantings on wheat cropland can be done only on that acreage voluntarily diverted below the farm's 1965 effective allotment.

WORLD WHEAT SITUATION AND OUTLOOK

Situation in Major Exporting Countries

Canada's Total
  Supply Down

        Canada's carryover for all wheat on August 1, 1964, was 461 million
bushels, 27 million below the level of a year earlier but 70 million above the
small 1962 carryover (table 28). The 1964 crop of 600 million bushels is
down 123 million from the 1963 record but still above the level of most recent
years. The combined production and carryover gives Canada a total supply of
1,061 million bushels for 1964-65, down some from last year but about equal to
the levels of the late 1950's. Based on a normal domestic use of 150 to 160
million bushels, Canada had about 900 million available for export and carryover at the beginning of the crop year. Exports of wheat and flour from the
beginning of the crop year through January were about 200 million bushels,
about 90 million below that period a year earlier. Much of this year's exports
have gone to Mainland China and other Communist countries.

France Expects
  Good Export Year

        The carryover of wheat in France on July 1, 1964, was about 92 million
bushels compared with the 119 million of a year earlier. Despite this reduction, the 1964 carryover was still above that of recent years. The 1964
production of 500 million bushels was comparable to the good 1962 harvest and
123 million above the poor 1963 crop. Total estimated supply for 1964-65,
including an allowance for imports, may be slightly over 600 million bushels.
With a normal domestic disappearance of around 340 million, France had about
270 million bushels available for export and carryover at the beginning of the
crop year (table 28).

        Information to date indicates that France may attain a record level of
exports during 1964-65. These increased exports can be attributed partly to
extensive sales to Communist countries and to advantages accrued under their
membership in the Common Market. These advantages not only provide for the
exclusion of foreign wheats but also enable France to subsidize their exports
with funds provided by other Common Market members.

Australia and Argentina
  Have Record Crops

        Recent reports from Australia indicate that wheat production for 1964-65
will exceed the 1963-64 record of 328 million bushels by 62 million. This,
combined with a carryover of 20 million as of December 1, 1964, gives Australia
a total supply of 410 million bushels. A normal domestic use of between 70
and 80 million bushels would leave 330 million available for export and
carryover for the 1964-65 crop year. Communist China and Western Europe have
imported large amounts of wheat from Australia in recent years. Excellent

crops in Western Europe this year have lessened their needs, compelling Australia to seek other outlets for its surplus grain.

Argentina's wheat crop for 1964-65 is estimated at a record 338 million bushels, 38 million above last year's previous record. This, combined with a 66-million-bushel carryover, would give a total supply of over 400 million. Domestic needs in recent years have been about 130 million bushels and the quantity available for export and carryover in the 1964-65 season is indicated at around 270 million bushels. Communist China, Brazil, and other countries have already contracted for about 30 percent of this amount (table 28).

World Trade

1963-64 Trade
Sets Record

World trade in wheat and flour reached a record of about 2,000 million bushels in 1963-64. This is about 420 million bushels above 1962-63 and about 270 million more than the previous record established in 1961-62.

This record level of trade followed the poor 1963 world wheat crop which was down substantially from the 1962 record harvest. Poor crops in Russia and Western Europe necessitated large imports of wheat and flour. Japan made heavy imports because of a below normal crop, and Communist China continued to make substantial imports.

Trade Lower in 1964-65

World trade in wheat and flour in 1964-65 is expected to be about 15 percent below the record of around 2 billion bushels of 1963-64.

Record world wheat production in 1964, with larger crops in many importing countries, will reduce import requirements. Russia and Western Europe have much improved crops this year, which have substantially cut their import needs. India, Japan, and Communist China continue to import large quantities of wheat.

France, with a large 1964 crop, is anticipating a record 1964-65 export year. Argentina and Australia, both with record crops, are actively competing for export markets. The United States and Canada, both with large crops, are not expected to reach last year's record export levels, but will maintain exports above average.

EEC Reaches Price Agreement

In December 1964, the European Common Market's Council of Ministers reached a decision on the unification of grain prices throughout the 6 member countries. The prices go into effect on July 1, 1967. The basic target prices for soft and durum wheat will be $2.89 and $3.40 per bushel, respectively. The new target prices represent about an 11 percent reduction from Germany's former prices and a 6 percent increase over France's previous target prices.

The new price level will lower prices in Germany—the chief importing country—by about 10 percent and raise prices in France—the chief exporting country—by as much as 20 percent from current levels. German wheat farmers will receive compensatory payments to offset the effect of the lower prices on their income. The increase in target prices, plus elimination of taxes and other assessments on French producers, is expected to raise farm income and encourage increased production.

1965 Winter Wheat Crop Conditions 1/

Prospects Favorable in Western Europe

In Western Europe grain crops have generally wintered well, and conditions for fall planting were favorable. Moisture conditions have been favorable and large acreages of winter wheat are reported; another large harvest is indicated.

In France, the area planted to winter wheat was unusually large, estimated at about 10.6 million acres, 6 percent larger than a year earlier. Growth is reported as well advanced. Production of winter wheat accounts for 90 to 95 percent of the total French harvest. Assuming normal winterkill, the 1965 harvest is now expected to be about equal to the 509-million-bushel record crop of 1962.

In West Germany, winter crops were protected by snowcover during cold weather in December. January rains balanced the limited moisture condition that existed in some areas last fall and crops appear in favorable condition. Good weather has prevailed in Italy and fall-sown grains appear promising. In Greece, rainfall has been below average and wheat acreage is reported 10 percent lower than last year. In Spain and Portugal, recent rains have been beneficial after a prolonged dry period and average crops are expected.

Belgium has had recent precipitation and crops are generally in satisfactory condition. In The Netherlands, a large wheat acreage is estimated for this year and the winter crop is developing well. The area sown to winter wheat in the United Kingdom is substantially larger than a year ago. After periods of heavy rain and snow, drier weather has facilitated fieldwork.

Eastern European Crop Prospects Less Favorable

Because of a mild winter with little snowcover in Eastern Europe, crop prospects appear somewhat less favorable than a year ago. Winter wheat acreages are slightly larger in Poland, East Germany, and Czechoslovakia, while they are about the same in Hungary, Rumania, and Bulgaria. However, in Yugoslavia plantings are about 15 percent below those of last year.

In the Soviet Union a normal winter wheat crop appears likely, based on current indications. In the Ukraine, a large proportion of the crop entered the winter in good condition and fertilizer was applied to a much larger area than previously. In most of the spring wheat area, soil moisture is at a less favorable level than last year although better than in most recent years.

1/ Prepared in the Grain and Feed Division, FAS.

Table 2.- Wheat: Estimated supply and distribution by classes,
United States, average 1957-61 and annual 1962-64

Item	Hard winter	Red winter	Hard spring	Durum	White	Total
	Mil. bu.	Mil. bu.	Mil. bu.	Mil. bu.	Mil. bu.	Mil. bu.
Average 1957-61						
Carryover, July 1	860	12	221	20	49	1,162
Production	687	179	171	27	161	1,225
Imports 1/	---	---	8	---	---	8
Supply	1,547	191	400	47	210	2,395
Exports 2/	335	45	42	5	120	547
Domestic disappearance 3/	264	131	139	24	45	603
Carryover, June 30	948	15	219	18	45	1,245
1962-63						
Carryover, July 1, 1962	1,085	24	187	5	21	1,322
Production	537	157	175	70	155	1,094
Imports 1/	---	---	5	---	---	5
Supply	1,622	181	367	75	176	2,421
Exports 2/	437	40	39	4	122	642
Domestic disappearance 3/	249	136	133	25	41	584
Carryover, June 30, 1963	936	5	195	46	13	1,195
1963-64 4/						
Carryover, July 1, 1963	936	5	195	46	13	1,195
Production	545	219	161	51	166	1,142
Imports 1/	---	---	4	---	---	4
Supply	1,481	224	360	97	179	2,341
Exports 2/	565	80	50	29	136	860
Domestic disappearance 3/	248	140	128	27	37	580
Carryover, June 30, 1964	668	4	182	41	6	901
1964-65 4/ 5/						
Carryover, July 1, 1964	668	4	182	41	6	901
Production	642	229	172	66	181	1,290
Imports 1/	---	---	4	---	---	4
Supply	1,310	233	358	107	187	2,195
Exports 2/	460	70	30	5	110	*675
Domestic disappearance 3/	268	143	130	27	47	615
Carryover, June 30, 1965	582	20	198	75	30	905

1/ Exclude imports for milling-in-bond and export as flour. 2/ Include
exports for relief or charity by individuals and private agencies. Include
relief shipments of bulgar beginning 1962-63. 3/ Wheat for food (including
military food use at home and abroad), feed, seed and industry. Includes
shipments to U. S. Territories. 4/ Preliminary. 5/ Imports and distribution
are projected. *May not be fully attained due to dook strike.

Note.-Figures by classes in this table, except production, are only approxi-
mations.

Table 3 .- Wheat and flour: Current indicators of export movement,
by program, coastal area and class of wheat,
July-January 1963-64 and 1964-65

Period, program and coastal area	Wheat (grain only)-Inspections for export 1/							Flour (wheat equivalent)-Registrations of export sales 2/
	Hard Winter	Red Winter	hard Spring	Durum	White	Mixed	Total	
	Mil. bu.	Mil. bu.	Mil. bu.	Mil. bu.	Mil. bu.	Mil. bu.	Mil. bu.	Mil. bu.
July-January 1963-64								
Commercial	51.5	47.1	18.6	4.7	37.9	1.3	161.1	14.3
Government Programs:								
CCC Credit	3.9	.2	.4	---	3/	---	4.5	---
Title I-P.L. 480	155.9	2.9	.4	---	39.2	.4	198.8	22.5
Title IV-P.L. 480	2.2	.7	.2	---	1.0	---	4.1	.5
A.I.D.	.1	---	.5	---	---	---	.6	.1
Barter	10.3	---	.9	---	---	---	11.2	---
Donations	10.2	3/	9.7	---	3/	---	19.9	26.6
Total	234.1	50.9	30.7	4.7	78.1	1.7	400.2	64.0
July-January 1964-65								
Commercial	28.2	11.0	6.4	1.1	17.3	.6	64.6	11.3
Government Programs:								
CCC Credit	.4	1.0	.3	---	---	---	1.7	---
Title I-P.L. 480	245.5	4.4	.1	---	16.5	---	266.5	21.5
Title IV-P.L. 480	8.0	15.4	.4	---	1.0	---	24.8	3/
A.I.D.	---	---	---	---	---	---	---	.4
Barter	4.2	---	---	---	---	---	4.2	.2
Donations	4.8	---	.1	---	---	---	4.9	25.7
Total	291.1	31.8	7.3	1.1	34.8	.6	366.7	59.1
July-January 1963-64								
Coastal areas:								
Great Lakes	1.3	18.8	11.9	3.1	3.2	---	38.3	
Atlantic	1.1	21.0	11.4	1.4	11.0	.5	46.4	N
Gulf	202.6	11.1	5.0	.2	---	.7	219.6	O
Pacific	29.1	---	2.4	---	63.9	.5	95.9	T
Total	234.1	50.9	30.7	4.7	78.1	1.7	400.2	A
July-January 1964-65								V
								A
								I
Coastal areas:								L
Great Lakes	.7	6.8	4.2	.5	.9	---	13.1	A
Atlantic	4.3	7.1	.7	.5	.5	---	13.1	B
Gulf	262.1	17.9	1.2	.1	---	.5	281.8	L
Pacific	24.0	---	1.2	---	33.4	.1	58.7	E
Total	291.1	31.8	7.3	1.1	34.8	.6	366.7	

1/ Based on weekly reports of inspection for export. Does not include rail or truck movement to Canada or Mexico.

2/ Registrations of sales under the Cash Payment Flour Export Program (GR-346) for period ending on Saturday nearest to end of month shown. Flour inspections are not available nor are registrations of flour broken down by class of wheat from which the flour was milled.

3/ Less than 50,000 bushels.

Table 4 .- Wheat: U. S. inspections for export, by programs
and country of destination, July-January 1963-64

COUNTRY	COMMERCIAL	CCC CREDIT	PL-480 TITLE I	BARTER	DONATIONS 1/	PL-480 TITLE IV	A.I.D.	TOTAL
				1,000 BUSHELS				
Canada 2/	25,749	-	-	-	-	-	-	25,749
Algeria	-	-	-	-	5,386	-	-	5,386
Barbados	20	-	-	-	-	-	-	20
Belgium	8,186	894	-	-	-	-	-	9,080
Brazil	-	-	13,502	7,543	1,280	-	-	22,325
Chile	-	-	-	-	-	1,008	-	1,008
Colombia	1,763	-	-	-	18	1,129	-	2,910
Congo Republic	-	-	37	-	-	-	-	37
Dom. Republic	390	-	-	385	-	-	-	775
El Salvador	749	-	-	-	-	-	-	749
Formosa	458	-	5,052	-	924	-	-	6,434
West Germany	6,596	99	-	-	-	-	-	6,695
Guatemala	1,132	101	-	-	92	-	-	1,325
Honduras	318	-	-	-	-	-	-	318
Hong Kong	100	-	-	-	-	-	-	100
India	-	-	88,012	-	813	-	-	88,825
Israel	-	-	4,904	-	-	-	-	4,904
Japan	41,161	-	-	-	-	-	-	41,161
Kenya	-	-	-	-	-	-	112	112
Korea	-	-	11,515	-	1,942	-	-	13,457
Madeira Is.	92	-	-	-	-	-	-	92
Netherlands	15,898	583	-	-	-	-	-	16,481
Nicaragua	257	-	-	-	-	-	-	257
Pakistan	-	-	40,437	-	309	-	453	41,199
Paraguay	-	-	798	-	-	-	-	798
Peru	480	-	-	2,080	-	-	-	2,560
Philippines	6,276	-	-	-	-	-	-	6,276
Poland	10,618	-	5,493	661	-	-	-	16,772
Singapore	37	-	-	-	-	-	-	37
Spain	3,804	-	-	-	-	-	-	3,804
Sudan	416	-	1,248	-	-	-	-	1,664
U.A.R.	-	-	18,481	-	-	-	-	18,481
United Kingdom	8,877	1,617	-	-	-	-	-	10,494
Venezuela	4,137	487	39	-	-	-	-	4,663
Yugoslavia	-	-	1,903	-	-	-	-	1,903
Nigeria	967	-	-	-	-	-	-	967
Turkey	-	-	5,672	-	-	-	-	5,672
West Africa	212	-	-	-	-	-	-	212
Angola	761	-	-	-	-	-	-	761
Portugal	2,082	-	-	-	-	613	-	2,695
Panama	410	-	-	-	-	-	-	410
Other	19,149	727	1,637	600	9,117	1,387	-	32,617
GRAND TOTAL	161,095	4,508	198,730	11,269	19,881	4,137	565	400,185

1/ Includes Title II and III. 2/ For transshipment.
Based on weekly reports of inspections for export by licensed grain inspectors
and does not include rail and truck movement to Canada or Mexico.

Table 5.- Wheat: U. S. inspections for export, by programs
and country of destination, July-January 1964-65

COUNTRY	COMMERCIAL	CCC CREDIT	PL-480 TITLE I	BARTER	DONATIONS 1/	PL-480 TITLE IV	A.I.D.	TOTAL
				1,000 BUSHELS				
LAKE PORTS								
Canada	8,587	-	-	-	-	-	-	8,587
Transshipments	7,727	-	-	-	-	1,574	-	9,301
2/ Difference	+860	0	0	0	0	-1,574	0	-714
Guatemala	719	-	-	280	87	-	-	1,086
El Salvador	420	-	-	-	-	-	-	420
Honduras	361	-	-	-	-	-	-	361
Panama	371	-	-	-	-	-	-	371
Chile	-	-	-	-	-	5,058	-	5,058
Haiti	431	453	-	-	-	-	-	884
Nicaragua	266	-	-	-	-	-	-	266
Colombia	766	-	-	1,625	-	-	-	2,391
Venezuela	5,350	37	-	-	-	-	-	5,387
Ecuador	222	-	105	-	-	468	-	795
Peru	92	-	454	665	-	424	-	1,635
Brazil	-	-	38,452	-	-	-	-	38,452
Soviet Union	1,677	-	-	-	-	-	-	1,677
United Kingdom	1,427	383	-	-	-	-	-	1,810
Turkey	-	-	5,499	-	-	-	-	5,499
Netherlands	6,122	-	-	-	-	-	-	6,122
France	710	-	-	-	-	-	-	710
Spain	1,023	-	-	-	-	-	-	1,023
West Germany	838	-	-	-	-	-	-	838
Poland	-	-	913	-	-	-	-	913
Portugal	564	-	1,133	-	-	1,097	-	2,794
Italy	2,693	-	-	-	-	-	-	2,693
Yugoslavia	-	-	1,968	-	-	17,646	-	19,614
Sudan	176	-	947	423	154	-	-	1,700
Iran	503	-	6,394	-	-	-	-	6,897
Israel	-	-	3,115	828	-	-	-	3,943
Afghanistan	-	-	-	-	198	-	-	198
India	-	-	132,020	52	461	-	-	132,533
Pakistan	-	-	38,843	32	119	1,269	-	40,263
Philippines	2,969	-	-	-	-	-	-	2,969
Korea	-	-	10,661	-	4	-	-	10,665
Canary Is.	884	-	-	-	-	-	-	884
Taiwan(Formosa)	1,719	-	5,986	-	130	-	-	7,835
Japan	28,380	-	-	-	-	-	-	28,380
Nigeria	1,436	-	-	-	-	-	-	1,436
U.A.R.(Egypt)	-	821	18,772	-	-	-	-	19,593
Greece	784	-	-	-	-	-	-	784
Other	2,824	-	1,233	322	3,723	385	-	8,487
GRAND TOTAL	64,587	1,694	266,495	4,227	4,876	24,773	0	366,652

1/ Includes Title II and III. 2/ Transshipments of U. S. wheat from Canada
were subtracted from quantity shipped to Canada to show country of destination
of U. S. wheat. If shipments to Canada are larger than transshipments, the
difference is added to the total inspections. If shipments are smaller than
transshipments, the difference (which indicates a reduction in U. S. wheat
stocks in Canada) is subtracted.

Table 6.- Wheat and rye: Farm, cash, export, and support prices at major markets and ports, per bushel, specified months and days, 1964-65 1/

Commodity and market	Monthly average price					Daily price comparisons					
	1964			1965		February 27, 1964			February 25, 1965		
	Oct.	Nov.	Dec.	Jan.	Feb. 2/	Price	Effective support 3/	Price above support	Price	Effective support 3/	Price above support
	Dol.	Dol.	Dol.	Dol.	Dol.	Dol.	Dol.	Dol.	Dol.	Dol.	Dol.
Wheat											
All wheat: U. S. average received by farmers	1.36	1.39	1.39	1.38	1.37	---	---	---	---	---	---
No. 1 Hard Red Winter											
Kansas City, ordinary protein	1.66	1.67	1.64	1.62	1.61	2.19	2.06	.13	1.58	1.52	.06
Kansas City, 13% protein	1.69	1.71	1.68	1.66	1.66	2.24	n.a.	n.a.	1.63	n.a.	n.a.
Gulf Ports, ord. protein, export	1.82	1.86	1.84	1.80	1.78	2.39	---	---	1.76	---	---
" " " , net export	1.87	1.85	1.83	1.80	1.65	1.80	---	---	1.69	---	---
Eastern Soft											
No. 2 Red Winter											
Chicago	1.52	1.55	1.52	1.53	1.53	2.13	2.08	.05	1.52	1.55	-.03
St. Louis	1.51	1.56	1.55	1.57	1.58	2.19	2.08	.11	1.57	1.55	.02
Baltimore, export	1.62	1.66	1.67	1.68	1.69	2.32	---	---	1.68	---	---
" , net export	1.67	1.65	1.66	1.68	1.56	1.73	---	---	1.54	---	---
No. 2 White, Toledo	1.44	1.45	1.46	1.45	1.45	2.09	---	---	1.45	---	---
No. 1 Dk. Northern Spring, Minneapolis											
Ordinary protein	1.75	1.78	1.77	1.78	1.78	2.22	2.15	.07	1.78	1.62	.16
13% protein	1.80	1.81	1.80	1.79	1.78	2.24	n.a.	n.a.	1.78	n.a.	n.a.
15% protein	1.81	1.82	1.80	1.79	1.79	2.25	n.a.	n.a.	1.79	n.a.	n.a.
No. 1 Hard Amber Durum, Minneapolis	1.69	1.70	1.66	1.67	1.63	2.27	2.40	-.13	1.61	1.72	-.11
White, Pacific Northwest											
No. 1 Soft, Portland	1.48	1.51	1.51	1.49	1.50	2.21	1.99	.22	1.50	1.46	.04
No. 2 Western, export	1.51	1.54	1.53	1.52	1.52	2.25	---	---	1.52	---	---
" " " , net export	1.71	1.70	1.66	1.61	1.51	1.78	---	---	1.50	---	---
Rye											
U. S. average received by farmers	1.03	1.02	.97	.94	.96	---	---	---	---	---	---
No. 2, Minneapolis	1.24	1.25	1.21	1.19	1.18	1.32	1.27	.05	1.76	1.27	-.11

1/ Cash grain prices are on-track cash prices established at the close of the market. The effective support price is the established terminal support less the storage charges to the maturity date of the price support loan. Export prices are basis prompt or 30-day shipment. Net export prices are derived by subtracting export payment rates. The export marketing certificate required since July 1, 1964 is included in the computation of the net export price. Wheat used for domestic prices shown. The export marketing certificate which is not included in the domestic prices shown. 2/ Preliminary. 3/ Not available for high-protein wheats since quality premiums are based on a combination of the sedimentation tests and the protein tests. Not applicable if market is not an established price support terminal or if the price is an export price.

Table 7.- Wheat: Weighted average cash price per bushel, specified markets and dates, October-February, 1963-64 and 1964-65

Month and week	All classes and grades, six markets		No. 1 Hard Winter, Kansas City		No. 1 Dark N. Spring, Minneapolis		No. 1 Hard Amber Durum, Minneapolis		No. 2 Soft Red Winter, St. Louis		No. 1 Soft White, Portland 1/	
	1963-1964	1964-1965	1963-1964	1964-1965	1963-1964	1964-1965	1963-1964	1964-1965	1963-1964	1964-1965	1963-1964	1964-1965
	Dol.	Dol.	Dol.	Dol.	Dol.	Dol.	Dol.	Dol.	Dol.	Dol.	Dol.	Dol.
Month												
October	2.37	1.75	2.21	1.68	2.43	1.84	2.50	1.76	---	---	2.15	1.48
November	2.34	1.75	2.22	1.69	2.39	1.84	2.47	1.75	2/2.16	2/1.52	2.17	1.51
December	2.31	1.71	2.23	1.66	2.37	1.82	2.42	1.75	3/2.21	2/1.58	2.17	1.50
January	2.31	1.70	2.25	1.64	2.37	1.80	2.41	1.74	3/2.28	2/1.57	2.25	1.49
Week ended												
October 16	2.38	1.73	2.21	1.69	2.44	1.82	2.50	1.75	---	---	2.16	1.47
23	2.35	1.77	2.21	1.71	2.42	1.85	2.46	1.79	---	---	2.15	1.48
30	2.36	1.75	2.23	1.67	2.44	1.84	2.51	1.75	---	---	2.17	1.50
November 6	2.36	1.75	2.22	1.68	2.42	1.84	2.48	1.76	---	2/1.52	2.16	1.50
13	2.33	1.76	2.23	1.68	2.39	1.85	2.48	1.75	---	---	2.17	1.50
20	2.33	1.73	2.20	1.68	2.37	1.83	2.45	1.75	---	---	2.17	1.51
27	2.34	1.74	2.21	1.70	2.38	1.84	2.48	1.75	2/2.16	---	2.17	1.50
December 4	2.32	1.74	2.22	1.68	2.35	1.83	2.43	1.75	---	---	2.15	1.51
11	2.29	1.72	2.23	1.68	2.36	1.81	2.40	1.75	2/2.19	---	2.16	1.51
18	2.29	1.71	2.23	1.67	2.38	1.81	2.42	1.76	2/2.23	---	2.17	1.50
25	2.32	1.70	2.24	1.64	2.40	1.83	2.41	1.75	---	---	2.18	1.50
January 1	2.32	1.71	2.25	1.63	2.38	1.83	2.44	1.75	---	2/1.58	2.21	1.50
8	2.33	1.69	2.26	1.64	2.39	1.80	2.42	1.74	---	---	2.25	1.49
15	2.32	1.69	2.25	1.64	2.37	1.80	2.41	1.73	2/2.28	2/1.57	2.27	1.50
22	2.30	1.70	2.25	1.63	2.36	1.81	2.39	1.75	---	---	2.24	1.49
29	2.27	1.70	2.24	1.63	2.35	1.80	2.35	1.74	2/2.29	---	2.26	1.49
February 5	2.28	1.71	2.24	1.64	2.34	1.82	2.42	1.73	---	2/1.56	2.26	1.50
12	2.28	1.69	2.25	1.63	2.32	1.80	2.41	1.72	2/2.31	---	2.24	1.50
19	2.28	1.67	2.25	1.62	2.32	1.79	2.36	1.70	---	1.51	2.25	1.50

1/ Average of daily cash quotations. 2/ 1 car sold. 3/ 2 cars sold.

Table 8.- Wheat: Average closing price per bushel of May future, specified markets and dates, October-February, 1963-64 and 1964-65

Month and week	Chicago		Kansas City		Minneapolis	
	1963-64	1964-65	1963-64	1964-65	1963-64	1964-65
	Dollars	Dollars	Dollars	Dollars	Dollars	Dollars
Month						
October	2.09	1.54	2.03	1.56	2.25	1.71
November	2.12	1.56	2.04	1.56	2.22	1.69
December	2.13	1.52	2.05	1.53	2.25	1.69
January	2.17	1.50	2.09	1.51	2.26	1.68
Week ended						
October 16	2.09	1.53	2.03	1.55	2.25	---
23	2.10	1.54	2.04	1.57	2.23	1.72
30	2.13	1.54	2.06	1.56	2.24	1.71
November 6	2.13	1.55	2.06	1.56	2.23	1.70
13	2.14	1.57	2.05	1.56	2.22	1.69
20	2.09	1.56	2.02	1.56	2.21	1.69
27	2.12	1.56	2.04	1.56	2.23	1.69
December 4	2.13	1.54	2.03	1.56	2.22	1.69
11	2.13	1.53	2.05	1.55	2.24	1.69
18	2.13	1.53	2.05	1.54	2.27	1.69
25	2.14	1.52	2.06	1.52	2.27	1.70
January 1	2.16	1.50	2.07	1.51	2.27	1.69
8	2.19	1.51	2.10	1.52	2.27	1.68
15	2.19	1.50	2.10	1.51	2.26	1.68
22	2.17	1.48	2.09	1.51	2.26	1.68
29	2.16	1.51	2.08	1.52	2.25	1.69
February 5	2.15	1.52	2.07	1.52	2.25	1.70
12	2.16	1.51	2.07	1.52	2.25	1.70
19	2.15	1.51	2.05	1.52	2.24	1.69

Table 9.— Wheat: Average price per bushel received by farmers, parity price, and price of Hard Winter at Kansas City, 1958-64

Year beginning July	July	Aug.	Sept.	Oct.	Nov.	Dec.	Jan.	Feb.	March	April	May	June	Average
	Dol.	Dol.	Dol.	Dol.	Dol.	Dol.	Dol.	Dol.	Dol.	Dol.	Dol.	Dol.	Dol.
					Price received by farmers on 15th of month 1/								
1958	64	1.	1.68	1.73	1.74	1.73	1.71	1.74	1.76	1.77	1.77	1.69	1.75
1959	70	1.	1.72	1.76	1.79	1.79	1.78	1.80	1.82	1.82	1.82	1.72	1.76
1960	67	1.	1.72	1.74	1.76	1.77	1.79	1.81	1.80	1.74	1.76	1.72	1.74
1961	73	1.	1.87	1.88	1.88	1.89	1.88	1.88	1.89	1.92	1.98	1.99	1.83
1962	98	2.	1.99	1.97	2.00	2.02	2.01	2.04	2.04	2.09	2.04	1.86	2.04
1963	75	1.64	1.84	1.95	1.95	1.97	2.00	1.99	1.85	1.94	1.88	1.40	1.85
1964	1.33	1.99	1.36	1.36	1.39	1.39	1.38	1.37					1.38
					Parity price 2/								
1958	2.44	.43	.43	2.42	2.44	.44	.36	2 36	2.36	2.37	2.37	2.36	
1959	2.36	.36	.36	2.35	2.36	.36	.37	2:37	2.38	2.39	2.38	2.37	
1960	2.36	.36	.36	2.35	2.35	.36	.38	2.39	2.39	2.39	2.39	2.37	
1961	2.37	.38	.38	2.38	2.38	.39	.43	2.43	2.43	2.44	2.43	2.42	
1962	2.42	2.42	2.44	2.44	2.44	2.45	2.49	2.49	2.49	2.49	2.51	2.51	
1963	2.51	.51	.51	2.51	2.51	.50	.52	2.52	2.52	2.53	2.52	2.52	
1964	2.51	.52	.52	2.51	2.52	.52	.52	2.53					
					Price of No. 1 Hard Winter, Kansas City 3/								
1958	1.84	1.85	1.95	1.97	2	1.98	2	2.03	2.07	2.09	2.03	1.92	1.94
1959	1.94	1.99	2.01	2.05	2	2.08	2:	2.10	2.12	2.10	2.01	1.95	2.00
1960	1.89	1.94	1.96	1.99	2	2.02	2.	2.05	2.02	2.00	1.96	1.92	1.94
1961	1.98	2.04	2.07	2.08	2	2.14	2.	2.11	2.12	2.13	2.17	2.19	2.05
1962	2.22	2.25	2.23	2.19	2	2.28	2.	2.30	2.33	2.37	2.28	2.03	2.25
1963 4/	2.01	2.05	2.11	2.21	2.00	2.23	2.08	2.24	2.18	2.27	2.17	1.55	2.00
1964	1.57	1.61	1.65	1.68	1.44	1.66	1.08	5/1.63					

1/ State monthly prices are weighted by estimated sales for the month to compute U. S. prices. State crop year averages, weighted by estimated sales, are used to obtain U. S. averages. Includes an allowance for unredeemed loans at average loan values. 2/ Through December 1958, transitional parity. Beginning January 1959, modernized parity. 3/ Compiled from the Kansas City Grain Market Review. Average of daily prices weighted by carlot sales. Sales of Dark Hard and Hard Winter wheat combined, reported as Hard Winter. 4/ Prior to July 1963, prices are for No. 2 Hard Winter. 5/ Preliminary.

Table 10.- Wheat: Stocks, United States, by quarters, 1958-65

Year	January 1					April 1				
	Farm	Terminal market 1/	Interior mill, elevator, and warehouse	Commodity Credit Corporation 2/	Total	Farm	Terminal market 1/	Interior mill, elevator, and warehouse	Commodity Credit Corporation 2/	Total
	1,000 bu.	1,000 bu.	1,000 bu.	1,000 bu.	1,000 bu.	1,000 bu.	1,000 bu.	1,000 bu.	1,000 bu.	1,000 bu.
1958	294,550	360,662	657,075	72,516	1,384,803	177,848	335,916	535,332	74,571	1,123,667
1959	456,849	422,047	854,305	87,230	1,820,431	283,447	419,579	761,126	77,029	1,541,181
1960	328,554	485,656	989,552	70,932	1,874,694	203,747	458,349	836,814	62,589	1,561,499
1961	422,055	3/	1,568,024	77,940	2,068,019	258,115	3/	1,376,245	72,259	1,706,619
1962	359,484	3/	1,562,774	60,305	1,982,563	211,652	3/	1,371,134	59,223	1,642,009
1963	316,483	3/	1,441,817	58,221	1,816,521	194,999	3/	1,262,190	46,903	1,504,092
1964	309,694	3/	1,273,455	30,633	1,613,782	153,433	3/	1,037,779	14,379	1,205,591
1965 4/	390,126	3/	1,041,284	11,134	1,442,544					
	July 1					October 1				
1958	51,193	304,782	447,128	78,270	881,373	643,550	472,590	940,838	83,731	2,140,709
1959	114,913	403,845	695,241	81,067	1,295,066	450,951	526,717	1,074,638	77,006	2,129,312
1960	95,935	411,976	742,156	63,451	1,313,518	550,606	3/	1,729,620	65,290	2,345,516
1961	136,937	3/	1,203,682	70,559	1,411,178	466,844	3/	1,786,432	63,554	2,316,830
1962	102,308	3/	1,160,015	59,547	1,321,870	406,243	3/	1,604,885	58,958	2,070,086
1963	95,254	3/	1,061,362	38,317	1,194,933	410,132	3/	1,498,593	34,028	1,942,753
1964 4/	75,477	3/	812,997	12,719	901,193	506,308	3/	1,293,069	12,586	1,811,963

1/ From reports of the Grain Division, Agricultural Marketing Service. 2/ Wheat owned by CCC and stored in bins or other storage owned or controlled by CCC. Other wheat owned by CCC as well as wheat outstanding under loan is included in other positions. 3/ Beginning October 1, 1960, terminal market included with interior mill, elevator and warehouse stocks. 4/ Preliminary.

Table 11.- Wheat: CCC operations and stocks, as of January 1965, with comparisons

Item	Price Support Activity		
	1963 crop through or as of-		1964 crop through or as of
	January 31, 1964	June 30, 1964	January 31, 1965
	Mil. bu.	Mil. bu.	Mil. bu.
Loan applications	---	---	292.6
Placed under loan:			
Warehouse stored	89.4	90.0	93.3
Farm stored	70.5	70.5	94.2
Total under loan	1/171.5	1/172.4	187.5
Loan repayments	58.9	84.9	31.4
Loan deliveries	---	1/ 65.0	---
Outstanding under loan	112.6	1.9	156.1
Remaining under reseal loan	64.3	52.0	51.7

	Sales and dispositions		
	July-Jan. 1963-64	July-June 1963-64	July-Jan. 1964-65
Statutory Minimum 2/	75.0	86.4	130.1
Domestic	7.8	15.2	15.6
Export			
Redemption of P.I.K.	93.8	162.7	64.4
Barter	21.4	33.7	6.4
GSM Credit	10.5	14.3	2.7
Donations	19.6	29.4	5.8
Total export	145.3	240.1	79.3
Total sales and dispositions	228.1	341.7	225.0

	Stocks owned by CCC		
Class of wheat	January 1, 1964	October 1, 1964	January 1, 1965
Hard Winter	755.9	580.7	510.7
Hard Spring	167.1	170.8	166.5
Red Winter	1.6	.5	.3
White	1.1	.7	.5
Durum	23.6	32.1	32.8
Mixed	1.1	1.2	.7
Total	950.4	786.0	711.5

1/ Includes purchase agreements. 2/ For unrestricted use.

Agricultural Stabilization and Conservation Service--Based on operating reports which differ from more complete fiscal reports.

Table 12.- Wheat and feed grain price relationships, per 100 pounds, averages July-September and October-December 1964

Region or State	Feed grain	July-September average		Wheat over feed grain		October-December average		Wheat over feed grain	
		Wheat	Feed grain	Actual	Adjusted for feed value 1/	Wheat	Feed grain	Actual	Adjusted for feed value 1/
		Dol.	Dol.	Dol.	Dol.	Dol.	Dol.	Dol.	Dol.
Soft Red Winter Wheat Region:									
Middle Atlantic 2/	Corn	2.21	2.49	-.28	-.41	2.28	2.37	-.09	-.21
South Atlantic 3/	"	2.24	2.33	-.09	-.21	2.32	2.18	.14	.03
East North Central 4/	"	2.20	2.06	.14	-.03	2.24	1.90	.34	.24
East South Central 5/	"	2.25	2.25	0	-.12	2.35	2.16	.19	.08
Western White Wheat States:									
Washington	Barley	2.23	1.92	.31	0	2.16	2.02	.14	-.19
Oregon	"	2.31	2.09	.22	-.12	2.21	2.22	-.01	-.37
Idaho	"	2.11	1.91	.20	-.11	2.12	2.01	.11	-.22
Hard Spring Wheat States:									
North Dakota	Barley	2.32	1.62	.70	.44	2.38	1.76	.62	.33
"	Oats	2.32	1.48	.84	.60	2.38	1.56	.82	.57
"	Rye	2.32	1.69	.63	.23	2.38	1.61	.77	.39
South Dakota	Oats	2.30	1.71	.59	.31	2.41	1.84	.57	.27
"	Corn	2.30	1.92	.38	.28	2.41	1.87	.54	.44
Montana	Barley	2.13	1.53	.60	.35	2.13	1.63	.50	.23
Hard Winter Wheat States:									
Kansas	Sorghum grain:	2.24	1.77	.47	.27	2.40	1.85	.55	.34
Oklahoma	" "	2.33	1.84	.49	.29	2.50	1.94	.56	.34
"	Barley	2.33	1.72	.61	.33	2.50	1.97	.53	.21
Texas	Sorghum grain:	2.41	1.81	.60	.40	2.53	1.91	.62	.41
"	Oats	2.41	2.34	.07	-.31	2.53	2.43	.10	-.30
Minnesota	Barley	2.48	1.76	.72	.43	2.60	1.84	.76	.46
"	Oats	2.48	1.76	.72	.43	2.60	1.85	.75	.45
Colorado	Corn	2.14	2.24	-.10	-.22	2.24	2.23	.01	-.11
Nebraska	Sorghum grain:	2.18	1.72	.46	.27	2.34	1.73	.61	.42
United States average	Corn	2.24	2.03	.21	.10	2.30	1.95	.35	.25
"	Barley	2.24	1.91	.33	.02	2.30	1.99	.31	-.01
"	Sorghum grain:	2.24	1.82	.42	.22	2.30	1.89	.41	.20
"	Oats	2.24	1.85	.39	.09	2.30	1.96	.34	.02
"	Rye	2.24	1.81	.43	.01	2.30	1.80	.50	.08

1/ Adjusted for feeding value of each grain, with wheat equal to 100 percent, 95 percent; sorghum grain 90.0 percent; oats and barley, 86.0 percent, and rye, 81.0 percent. Consumption of feed by livestock, Production Research Report No. 79, ERS, USDA. 2/ Includes N. Y., N. J., and Penn. 3/ u.Includes Del., Md., Va., W. Va., N. C., S. C., Ga., and Fla. 4/ Ides Ohio, Ind., Ill., Mich., and Wis. 5/ Includes Ky., Tenn., Ala., and Miss.

Table 13.- Eastern Soft wheat: Estimated supply and disappearance,
year beginning July, 1957-64 1/

Item	1957	1958	1959	1960	1961	1962	1963	1964
	Mil. bu.	Mil. bu.	Mil. bu.	Mil. bu.	Mil. bu.	Mil. bu.	Mil. bu.	Mil. bu.
Supply								
Carryover, July 1	13	8	25	14	16	29	7	5
Production	187	237	194	226	244	189	256	266
Total	200	245	219	240	260	218	263	271
Disappearance								
Exports, grain only								
Commercial	5	26	19	31	58	34	85	---
Government	32	37	38	32	16	17	10	---
Total	37	63	57	63	74	51	95	80
Domestic disappearance								
(including export flour)	155	157	148	161	157	160	163	166
Total disappearance	192	220	205	224	231	211	258	246
Carryover, June 30	8	25	14	16	29	7	5	25

1/ The bulk of the Michigan crop and all of the New York crop are white wheat and all stocks in Michigan are white. The data on white wheat are totaled with the soft red winter, shown regularly in the Wheat Situation, to obtain these estimates.

Table 14.- Winter wheat: Seedings and production in major-producing States, average 1959-63, annual 1964 and 1965

State	Acreage seeded for crop of- 1/				Production		
	Average 1959-63	1964	1965 2/	1965 as percentage of 1964	Average 1959-63	1964	1965 2/
	1,000 acres	1,000 acres	1,000 acres	Percent	1,000 bushels	1,000 bushels	1,000 bushels
Major Soft Winter States:							
Ohio	1,443	1,417	1,261	89	43,715	45,309	41,613
Indiana	1,303	1,476	1,269	86	42,434	51,465	46,953
Illinois	1,708	1,852	1,704	92	53,983	66,822	61,344
Michigan	1,084	1,017	895	88	35,893	39,273	31,325
Missouri	1,458	1,621	1,556	96	36,632	46,442	45,124
Major Hard Winter States:							
Kansas	10,517	10,641	11,492	108	235,298	215,460	241,332
Oklahoma	4,770	4,882	5,321	109	93,838	96,623	122,383
Texas	3,918	4,002	4,162	104	61,041	61,848	66,592
Montana	2,172	2,045	2,618	128	43,130	52,269	60,214
Colorado	2,587	2,761	2,954	107	46,782	27,296	17,724
Nebraska	3,282	3,235	3,461	107	69,885	73,825	72,681
Pacific Northwest:							
Washington	1,832	1,863	2,161	116	61,555	75,726	82,118
Oregon	724	744	781	105	23,689	25,660	22,649
Idaho	739	782	860	110	20,188	26,400	27,520
Others	4,549	4,903	4,622		98,497	120,470	102,484
United States	42,086	43,241	45,117	104.3	966,560	1,024,888	1,042,056

1/ Total acreage seeded for all purposes in preceeding fall.
2/ Indicated December 1, 1964.

Table 15.- Wheat, 1964 crop: Price support loan applications and activity, as of January 31, 1965

State	Approved for price support 1/		Put under loan through January 31	Remaining eligible for loan as of January 31 2/	Outstanding under loan on January 31		
	Applications	Quantity			Warehouse stored	Farm stored	Total
	Number	1,000 bu.	1,000 bu.	1,000 bu.	1,000 bu.	1,000 bu.	1,000 bu.
Alabama	3	11.8	5.3	6.5	4.5	--	4.5
Arizona	1	5.7	4.7	1.0	--	4.7	4.7
Arkansas	68	212.2	198.4	13.8	163.0	28.7	191.7
California	27	294.9	245.2	49.7	81.1	137.6	218.7
Colorado	577	2,741.3	1,790.3	951.0	210.5	1,157.6	1,368.1
Delaware	35	38.4	34.8	3.6	31.3	3.1	34.4
Georgia	156	319.0	246.9	72.1	40.3	92.1	132.4
Idaho	1,761	9,795.1	6,800.5	2,994.6	3,964.6	2,185.9	6,150.5
Illinois	1,049	1,377.2	1,178.3	198.9	660.4	311.4	971.8
Indiana	777	832.3	670.3	162.0	390.7	174.1	564.8
Iowa	45	76.3	68.7	7.6	26.2	3.7	29.9
Kansas	23,185	55,691.8	36,955.5	18,736.3	19,696.8	4,538.6	24,235.4
Kentucky	337	449.1	423.0	26.1	262.4	102.5	364.9
Louisiana	2	17.5	15.7	1.8	--	--	--
Maryland	343	383.0	378.6	4.4	377.0	1.4	378.4
Michigan	1,839	2,666.2	1,745.2	321.0	1,120.1	493.4	1,613.5
Minnesota	2,516	4,535.8	2,779.0	1,756.8	381.3	2,154.4	2,535.7
Mississippi	--	7.0	6.3	.7	2.5	--	2.5
Missouri	1,587	2,038.0	1,770.9	267.1	1,204.2	318.3	1,522.5
Montana	3,994	27,600.4	15,940.4	11,660.0	844.7	13,995.9	14,840.6
Nebraska	8,225	15,650.4	11,187.6	4,462.8	3,953.2	5,639.3	9,592.5
Nevada	3	26.9	23.0	3.9	--	23.0	23.0
Nw Jersey	113	214.2	176.6	37.6	116.0	57.5	173.5
Nw Mexico	73	453.2	371.8	81.4	249.2	10.9	260.1
Nw York	815	1,022.4	793.5	228.9	196.7	577.6	774.3
North Carolina	106	82.0	71.4	10.6	3.4	53.8	57.2
North Dakota	26,588	89,674.8	46,351.5	43,323.3	5,967.2	37,709.7	43,676.9
Ohio	2,191	2,048.7	1,903.3	145.4	1,371.6	178.9	1,550.5
Oklahoma	4,132	12,789.7	9,137.8	3,651.9	3,803.5	551.3	4,354.8
Oregon	1,276	9,200.6	8,242.4	958.2	5,461.6	2,383.0	7,844.6
Pennsylvania	417	298.3	286.3	12.0	231.5	43.7	275.2
South Carolina	78	114.1	96.2	17.9	54.2	12.0	66.2
South Dakota	6,377	17,751.4	11,521.5	6,229.9	1,980.8	8,382.3	10,363.1
Tennessee	102	130.6	123.5	7.1	63.4	23.2	86.6
Texas	, 71	6,465.0	5,424.8	1,040.2	3,419.1	132.8	3,551.9
Utah	58	226.7	139.6	87.1	15.6	109.7	125.3
Virginia	276	212.4	200.7	11.7	105.9	23.9	129.8
Washington	3,286	27,050.3	19,732.7	7,317.6	13,429.8	4,282.0	17,711.8
Wisconsin	41	35.4	31.4	4.0	15.6	15.8	31.4
Wyoming	124	611.9	378.8	233.1	16.5	240.2	256.2
Total	93,757	292,552.0	187,452.4	105,099.6	69,916.4	86,154.0	156,070.4

1/ Through the close of the application period, January 31. 2/ mers had through February 28 to put any additional or all of this wheat under loan.

Agricultural Stabilization and Conservation Service, Policy and Program Appraisal Division.

Table 16.- Wheat: Computation of blend price received by farmers
and value, 1963 and 1964, with comparisons

Item	Unit	Year beginning July		
		1962	1963	1964 1/
Average price received by farmers in the market 2/	Dol. per bu.	2.04	1.85	1.38
Average allowance for direct payments	" " "	---	.07	.31
Blend price received by farmers	" " "	2.04	1.92	1.69
Value of production	Mil. dol.	2,228	2,116	1,774
Price support payments	" "	---	79	---
Marketing certificate payments	" "	---	---	410
Gross value of the crop 3/	" "	2,228	2,195	2,184

1/ Preliminary.
2/ Includes allowance for unredeemed price support loan and purchase agree-
ment deliveries--no purchase agreements in 1964.
3/ Does not include acreage diversion payments since these do not relate to
production.

Table 17.- Grains: Price support loan rates and payments
per bushel, 1964 and 1965 crops

Grain	1964			1965		
	Loan rate	Direct payment	Total support	Loan rate	Direct payment	Total support
	Dol.	Dol.	Dol.	Dol.	Dol.	Dol.
Wheat	1.30	1/ .43	1.73	1.25	2/ .44	1.69
Rye	1.07	---	1.07	1.02	---	1.02
Corn	1.10	.15	1.25	1.05	.20	1.25
Barley	.84	.12	.96	.80	.16	.96
Grain Sorghum	.99	.13	1.12	.92	.20	1.12
Oats	.65	---	.65	.60	---	.60

1/ Payments on normal production as follows: 70 cents on 45 percent, 25
cents on 45 percent and 0 on 10 percent.
2/ Payments on normal production as follows: 75 cents on 45 percent, 30
cents on 35 percent and 0 on 20 percent.

Table 18.- Wheat and flour: Price relationships at milling centers,
year beginning July, 1957-64

Year and month	At Kansas City					At Minneapolis				
	Cost of wheat to produce 100 lb. of flour 1/	Wholesale price of-				Cost of wheat to produce 100 lb. of flour 1/	Wholesale price of-			
		Bakery flour per 100 lb. 2/	Byprod-ucts obtained 100 lb. flour 3/	Total products			Bakery flour per 100 lb. 2/	Byprod-ucts obtained 100 lb. flour 3/	Total products	
				Ac-tual	Over cost of wheat				Ac-tual	Over cost of wheat
	Dol.	Dol.	Dol.	Dol.	Dol.	Dol.	Dol.	Dol.	Dol.	Dol.
1957-58	5.18	5.64	.57	6.21	1.03	5.40	6.10	.57	6.67	1.27
1958-59	4.81	5.14	.63	5.77	.96	5.02	5.68	.64	6.32	1.30
1959-60	4.83	5.03	.60	5.63	.80	5.11	5.44	.61	6.05	.94
1960-61	4.77	5.04	.58	5.62	.85	4.92	5.36	.61	5.97	1.05
1961-62	5.13	5.37	.58	5.95	.82	5.43	5.70	.61	6.31	.88
1962-63	5.47	5.65	.68	6.33	.86	5.61	5.92	.68	6.60	.99
1963-64	4.99	5.25	.67	5.92	.93	5.20	5.52	.66	6.18	.98
1962-63										
July	5.40	5.82	.60	6.42	1.02	5.56	6.11	.59	6.70	1.14
August	5.47	5.93	.64	6.57	1.10	5.47	6.18	.61	6.79	1.32
September	5.43	5.85	.64	6.49	1.06	5.52	6.11	.63	6.74	1.22
October	5.45	5.75	.72	6.47	1.02	5.61	6.06	.70	6.76	1.15
November	5.52	5.77	.80	6.57	1.05	5.68	6.00	.79	6.79	1.11
December	5.52	5.65	.81	6.46	.94	5.65	5.86	.84	6.70	1.05
January	5.54	5.48	.81	6.29	.75	5.63	5.76	.83	6.59	.96
February	5.63	5.55	.74	6.29	.66	5.65	5.82	.75	6.57	.92
March	5.68	5.52	.63	6.15	.47	5.61	5.79	.69	6.48	.87
April	5.65	5.77	.55	6.32	.67	5.61	5.91	.60	6.51	.90
May	5.38	5.53	.56	6.09	.71	5.47	5.78	.59	6.37	.90
June	4.95	5.23	.62	5.85	.90	5.65	5.65	.61	6.26	.61
1963-64										
July	4.77	4.97	.69	5.66	.89	5.24	5.39	.64	6.03	.79
August	4.83	4.90	.67	5.57	.74	5.02	5.01	.64	5.65	.63
September	5.04	5.28	.74	6.02	.98	5.29	5.55	.68	6.23	.94
October	5.22	5.47	.71	6.18	.96	5.45	5.72	.65	6.37	.92
November	5.18	5.45	.75	6.20	1.02	5.38	5.74	.70	6.44	1.06
December	5.20	5.23	.81	6.04	.84	5.36	5.52	.81	6.33	.97
January	5.22	5.25	.74	5.99	.77	5.31	5.54	.72	6.26	.95
February	5.18	5.30	.63	5.93	.75	5.20	5.56	.61	6.17	.97
March	5.06	5.15	.61	5.76	.70	5.06	5.31	.61	5.92	.86
April	5.24	5.40	.66	6.06	.82	5.13	5.60	.67	6.27	1.14
May	5.11	5.25	.53	5.78	.67	5.29	5.48	.56	6.04	.75
June	3.97	5.33	.57	5.90	1.93	4.70	5.78	.60	6.38	1.68
1964-65										
July	5.34	5.64	.58	6.22	.88	5.52	5.98	.59	6.57	1.05
August	5.40	5.51	.62	6.13	.73	5.52	5.77	.59	6.36	.84
September	5.47	5.49	.66	6.15	.68	5.61	5.67	.63	6.30	.69
October	5.45	5.49	.69	6.18	.73	5.71	5.74	.68	6.42	.71
November	5.49	5.48	.70	6.18	.69	5.73	5.77	.68	6.45	.72
December	5.43	5.39	.86	6.25	.82	5.70	5.62	.82	6.44	.74
January	5.38	4/5.39	.77	6.16	.78	5.68	4/5.61	.75	6.36	.68

1/ Cost of 2.28 bushels: No. 1 Hard Winter, 13 percent protein, at Kansas City and simple average
of No. 1 Dark Northern Spring, 13 percent protein and 15 percent protein, at Minneapolis. Based on 73
percent extraction rate. Includes the 70-cent certificate beginning July 1964.
2/ Quoted as 95 percent patent at Kansas City and standard patent at Minneapolis, bulk basis.
3/ Assumes 50-50 millfeed distribution between bran and shorts or middlings, bulk basis.
4/ Preliminary.

Compiled from reports of the Agricultural Marketing Service and the Bureau of Labor Statistics,
Department of Labor.

Table 19.- Flour, wheat: Supply and distribution, United States, 1950-64

Calendar year	Production (Commercial and non-commercial) 1/	Imports of dutiable flour and products	Breakfast food made from flour (deduct)	Total flour supply	Exports: Flour 2/	Other products 3/	Shipments to Territories 4/	Military 5/	Civilian consumption: Total	Per capita
	1,000 cwt.	1,000 cwt.	1,000 cwt.	1,000 cwt.	1,000 cwt.	1,000 cwt.	1,000 cwt.	1,000 cwt.	1,000 cwt.	Lb.
1950	226,131	48	88	226,091	19,610	211	1,602	2,221	202,447	135
1951	230,468	50	88	230,430	22,959	198	1,662	1,815	200,796	133
1952	229,267	43	88	229,222	20,897	248	1,584	4,918	201,575	131
1953	223,247	88	88	223,247	17,347	243	1,670	4,642	199,345	128
1954	222,392	85	86	222,389	16,888	256	1,596	3,944	199,705	126
1955	226,500	91	88	226,503	21,547	317	1,631	3,665	199,343	123
1956	230,490	98	88	230,500	24,800	343	1,643	3,829	199,885	121
1957	239,551	95	88	239,558	33,995	526	1,648	3,189	200,200	119
1958	248,580	121	86	248,613	35,168	491	1,722	3,395	207,837	121
1959	251,075	145	88	251,132	37,159	518	1,312	2,888	209,255	120
1960	255,596	141	88	255,649	41,982	487	487	2,927	209,766	118
1961	260,746	131	88	260,789	43,294	502	481	2,714	213,798	118
1962	262,483	132	88	262,527	47,684	371	393	2,860	211,219	115
1963	264,265	136	88	264,313	44,439	1,085	353	2,822	215,614	116
1964 7/	265,885	142	88	265,939	42,349	893	320	2,430	219,947	116

1/ Commercial production of wheat flour (reported by Census), including flour milled in bond from foreign wheat plus the estimated flour equivalent of farm wheat ground or exchanged for flour for farm household use, as reported by SRS.
2/ Commercial deliveries for export, including milled-in-bond flour made from imported wheat, USDA procurement for export, and exports for relief of charity by individuals and private agencies.
3/ Commercial deliveries for export and USDA procurement for export of semolina, macaorni and bakery products in terms of flour.
4/ Exclude shipments to Alaska and Hawaii, beginning 1960.
5/ Includes other products in terms of flour in addition to flour per se. Covers supplies for civilian relief feeding in occupied areas as well as those for direct use of U.S. Armed Forces here and abroad.
6/ On a 50-State basis, beginning 1960.
7/ Preliminary.

Table 20.- Wheat ground and used for food, flour produced and consumed, United States, by half-years and calendar years, 1960-64

Period	Wheat ground for flour 1/					Flour produced 1/				
	1960	1961	1962	1963	1964 2/	1960	1961	1962	1963	1964 2/
	1,000 bu.	1,000 bu.	1,000 bu.	1,000 bu.	1,000 bu.	1,000 cwt.	1,000 cwt.	1,000 cwt.	1,000 cwt.	1,000 cwt.
January	50,471	51,562	53,532	50,248	53,494	22,061	22,678	23,515	22,116	23,519
February	47,038	48,251	49,417	47,017	47,862	20,575	21,284	21,738	20,700	21,218
March	51,053	51,499	52,606	50,550	49,646	22,331	22,722	23,165	22,296	21,956
April	44,656	42,492	46,225	49,005	50,226	19,519	18,744	20,421	21,570	22,241
May	43,850	47,199	48,021	51,105	49,897	19,207	20,793	21,175	22,542	21,961
June	46,526	46,276	45,677	46,520	61,557	20,359	20,381	20,125	20,421	27,057
January-June	283,594	287,279	295,478	294,445	312,682	124,052	126,602	130,139	129,645	137,952
July	44,482	47,310	46,130	49,215	34,215	19,420	20,782	20,334	21,687	14,953
August	50,810	54,454	52,865	51,990	47,324	22,194	23,810	23,207	22,886	20,818
September	49,801	48,118	48,371	48,798	52,968	21,805	21,112	21,254	21,409	23,305
October	53,610	52,480	54,140	56,105	56,460	23,496	23,063	23,807	24,649	25,017
November	50,837	52,250	51,743	50,558	50,765	22,374	22,933	22,744	22,220	22,407
December	49,585	50,108	46,626	48,599	47,910	21,800	22,014	20,584	21,399	21,104
July-December	299,125	304,720	299,875	305,265	289,642	131,089	133,714	131,930	134,250	127,604
Calendar year	582,719	591,999	595,353	599,710	602,324	255,141	260,316	262,069	263,895	265,556
	Wheat used for food in U.S. 3/					Flour consumed in U.S. 3/				
January-June	236,513	236,747	233,430	239,218	266,525	101,439	102,481	100,975	103,426	115,655
July-December	251,698	258,153	255,027	259,598	241,615	108,327	111,317	110,244	112,188	104,292
Calendar year	488,211	494,900	488,457	498,816	508,140	209,766	213,798	211,219	215,614	219,947

1/ Bureau of the Census data representing the grindings and production of all commercial mills in the United States. About 97 percent of the total was reported by 284 mills having a daily capacity of 401 sacks or more and the balance estimated. The estimated portion is based on the 1958 Census of Manufacturers.
2/ Preliminary.
3/ Excludes wheat used for food and flour consumed in the Territories and by our armed services at home and abroad. 50-State basis.

Table 21.- Wheat: Supply and disappearance, United States, annual 1955-64, and July-December and January-June periods, 1958-64

Year beginning July	Supply				Disappearance — Continental United States					Military procurement 4/	Exports 5/	Shipments 6/	Total
	Carry-over	Production	Imports 1/	Total	Civilian food 2/	Seed	Industrial	Feed 3/	Total				
	1,000 bu.	1,000 bu.	1,000 bu.	1,000 bu.	1,000 bu.	1,000 bu.	1,000 bu.	1,000 bu.	1,000 bu.	1,000 bu.	1,000 bu.	1,000 bu.	1,000 bu.
Annual													
1955	1,036,178	937,094	9,933	1,983,205	469,137	68,056	678	53,143	591,314	8,213	346,273	3,918	949,718
1956	1,033,487	1,005,397	7,783	2,046,667	469,736	57,995	497	47,397	575,625	8,636	549,536	4,040	1,137,837
1957	908,830	955,740	10,947	1,875,517	474,531	62,960	276	41,976	579,743	7,605	402,918	3,878	994,144
1958	881,373	1,457,435	7,769	2,346,577	485,651	64,287	134	46,863	596,915	7,372	443,294	3,930	1,051,511
1959	1,295,066	1,121,118	7,410	2,423,594	488,177	62,864	86	40,776	591,903	6,525	510,239	1,409	1,110,076
1960	1,313,518	1,357,272	8,232	2,679,022	488,445	63,963	83	45,725	598,216	6,433	661,945	1,250	1,267,844
1961	1,411,178	1,234,743	5,885	2,651,806	491,583	55,968	64	54,391	602,006	6,855	719,862	1,213	1,329,936
1962	1,321,870	1,093,667	5,556	2,421,093	494,245	60,610	71	21,379	576,305	6,500	642,300	1,055	1,226,160
1963 7/	1,194,933	1,142,013	4,329	2,341,275	526,123	62,776	56	*-15,396	573,559	5,600	859,520	1,403	1,440,082
1964 7/	901,193	1,290,468	4,000	2,195,00									
Half years													
1959													
July-Dec.	1,295,066	1,121,118	2,857	2,419,041	251,664	47,148	39	35,664	334,515	3,110	205,941	781	544,347
Jan.-June	1,874,694	—	4,553	1,879,247	236,513	15,716	47	5,112	257,388	3,415	94,298	628	565,729
1960													
July-Dec.	1,313,518	1,357,272	2,906	2,673,696	251,698	48,700	39	2,303	302,740	3,359	298,930	648	605,677
Jan.-June	2,068,019	—	5,326	2,073,345	236,747	15,263	44	43,422	295,476	3,074	363,015	602	662,167
1961													
July-Dec.	1,411,178	1,234,743	2,031	2,647,952	258,153	42,553	28	8/-7,053	293,681	3,241	367,801	666	665,389
Jan.-June	1,982,563	—	3,854	1,986,417	233,430	13,415	36	61,444	308,325	3,614	352,061	547	664,547
1962													
July-Dec.	1,321,870	1,093,667	1,485	2,417,022	255,027	46,936	34	14,772	316,769	3,000	280,200	532	600,501
Jan.-June	1,816,521	—	4,071	1,820,592	239,218	13,674	37	6,607	259,536	3,500	362,100	523	625,659
1963 7/													
July-Dec.	1,194,933	1,242,013	1,257	2,338,203	259,598	48,154	19	23,080	330,851	2,850	390,230	490	724,421
Jan.-June	1,613,782	—	3,072	1,616,854	266,525	14,622	37	*-38,476	242,708	2,750	469,290	913	715,661
1964 7/													
July-Dec.	901,193	1,290,468	780	2,192,441	243,614	49,500	37	62,646	353,797	2,800	392,800	500	749,897
Jan.-June	1,442,544	—											

1/ Include full-duty wheat, wheat imported for feed, and dutiable flour and other products in terms of wheat. Exclude wheat imported for milling in bond and export as flour, also flour free for export. 2/ Excludes shipments to United States Territories, and wheat for military food use at home and abroad. 3/ This is the residual figure, after all other disappearance has been taken into account. 4/ Takings for military food use at home and abroad. 5/ Include flour wholly from U. S. wheat and other products in terms of wheat. Include exports for relief or charity by individuals and private agencies. 6/ Shipments are to United States Territories. 7/ Preliminary. 8/ Known disappearance is larger than that indicated by January 1 stocks.

*See note at bottom of Table 1.

Table 22.- Wheat: Supply and disappearance, United States, July-December and January-June periods, 1948-58

Period	Supply				Disappearance									
					Continental United States					Military procure-ment 4/	Exports 5/	Shipments 6/	Total
	Carry-over	Produc-tion	Imports 1/	Total	Civilian food 2/	Seed	Indus-trial	Feed 3/	Total				
	1,000 bu.	1,000 bu.	1,000 bu.	1,000 bu.	1,000 bu.	1,000 bu.	1,000 bu.	1,000 bu.	1,000 bu.	1,000 bu.	1,000 bu.	1,000 bu.	1,000 bu.
Half years 1948													
July-Dec.	195,943	1,294,911	48	1,490,902	248,436	67,703	92	34,150	350,381	107,588	166,557	1,831	626,357
Jan.-June	864,545	---	1,482	866,027	223,047	27,312	101	71,198	321,658	73,930	161,270	1,804	558,742
1949													
July-Dec.	307,285	1,098,415	182	1,405,882	250,517	57,123	100	24,105	331,845	102,543	69,248	1,938	505,574
Jan.-June	900,308	---	2,055	902,363	233,665	23,728	92	87,153	344,638	20,983	109,965	2,063	477,649
1950													
July-Dec.	424,734	1,019,344	2,243	1,446,301	247,206	60,724	98	18,085	326,113	16,566	99,299	1,827	443,805
Jan.-June	1,002,496	---	9,676	1,012,172	232,314	27,180	94	90,723	350,341	24,701	235,214	2,045	612,301
1951													
July-Dec.	399,871	988,161	17,434	1,405,466	246,254	61,793	727	16,824	325,598	9,371	234,608	1,998	551,575
Jan.-June	853,891	---	24,175	868,066	234,830	26,402	203	85,577	347,012	7,343	255,739	1,994	612,088
1952													
July-Dec.	255,978	1,306,440	17,669	1,580,087	245,371	61,891	73	743	308,078	6,307	154,436	1,818	470,639
Jan.-June	1,109,448	---	3,933	1,113,381	228,242	27,200	102	81,737	337,281	7,313	161,216	2,027	507,837
1953													
July-Dec.	605,544	1,173,071	1,581	1,780,196	243,728	49,329	101	36,567	329,725	6,154	108,047	2,029	445,955
Jan.-June	1,334,241	---	3,956	1,338,197	228,934	20,149	77	40,070	289,230	5,880	107,657	1,924	404,691
1954													
July-Dec.	933,506	983,900	885	1,918,291	244,239	47,296	64	16,004	307,603	5,258	122,286	1,939	437,086
Jan.-June	1,481,205	---	3,312	1,484,517	226,810	17,492	166	44,063	290,531	4,624	151,333	2,651	448,339
1955													
July-Dec.	1,036,178	937,094	3,174	1,976,446	242,723	48,320	202	8/-10,075	281,170	3,926	121,987	1,903	408,986
Jan.-June	1,567,460	---	6,759	1,574,219	226,714	19,736	476	63,218	310,144	4,287	224,286	2,015	540,732
1956													
July-Dec.	1,033,487	1,005,397	3,043	2,041,927	241,640	42,336	291	13,857	298,124	4,657	248,210	1,960	552,951
Jan.-June	1,488,976	---	4,740	1,493,716	228,096	15,659	206	33,540	277,501	3,979	301,326	2,000	584,886
1957													
July-Dec.	908,830	955,740	5,263	1,869,833	241,624	48,479	182	8/-5,358	284,927	3,463	194,760	1,880	485,030
Jan.-June	1,384,803	---	5,684	1,390,487	232,907	14,481	94	47,334	294,816	4,142	208,158	1,998	509,114
1958													
July-Dec.	881,373	1,457,435	3,047	2,341,855	251,186	48,215	58	11,301	310,760	3,749	204,815	2,100	521,424
Jan.-June	1,820,431	---	4,722	1,825,153	234,465	16,072	56	35,562	286,155	3,623	238,479	1,830	530,087

See table 21 for footnotes.

Table 23.--All wheat, winter, and spring: Acreage, yield and production, United States, 1953-65

Year of harvest	All wheat				Winter wheat			
	Acreage		Yield per harvested acre	Production	Acreage		Yield per harvested acre	Production
	Planted	Harvested			Planted	Harvested		
	1,000 acres	1,000 acres	bushels	1,000 bushels	1,000 acres	1,000 acres	Bushels	1,000 bushels
1953	78,931	67,840	17.3	1,173,071	57,087	46,933	18.9	885,032
1954	62,539	54,356	18.1	983,900	46,617	39,218	20.4	801,369
1955	58,246	47,290	19.8	937,094	44,297	33,707	20.9	705,636
1956	60,655	49,768	20.2	1,005,397	44,418	35,532	20.8	740,592
1957	49,843	43,754	21.8	955,740	37,420	31,670	22.5	711,798
1958	56,017	53,047	27.5	1,457,435	43,674	41,023	28.6	1,173,538
1959	56,772	51,781	21.7	1,121,118	43,615	39,562	23.2	917,752
1960	54,919	51,896	26.2	1,357,272	42,689	39,996	27.8	1,110,557
1961	55,664	51,551	24.0	1,234,743	43,409	40,699	26.4	1,075,005
1962	49,132	43,541	25.1	1,093,667	38,733	33,576	24.5	820,998
1963	52,989	45,209	25.3	1,142,013	41,983	34,572	26.3	908,488
1964 1/	55,046	49,170	26.2	1,290,468	43,241	37,715	27.2	1,024,888
1965 2/					45,117			1,042,056

Year of harvest	All spring wheat				Durum				Spring other than durum			
	Acreage		Yield per harvested acre	Production	Acreage		Yield per harvested acre	Production	Acreage		Yield per harvested acre	Production
	Planted	Harvested			Planted	Harvested			Planted	Harvested		
	1,000 acres	1,000 acres	Bushels	1,000 bushels	1,000 acres	1,000 acres	Bushels	1,000 bushels	1,000 acres	1,000 acres	Bushels	1,000 bushels
1953	21,844	20,907	13.8	288,039	2,103	1,865	7.0	12,967	19,741	19,042	14.4	275,072
1954	15,922	15,138	12.1	182,531	1,637	1,309	3.8	4,982	14,285	13,829	12.8	177,549
1955	13,949	13,583	17.0	231,458	1,385	1,348	14.5	19,580	12,564	12,235	17.3	211,878
1956	16,237	14,236	18.6	264,805	2,489	2,318	16.7	38,791	13,748	11,918	19.0	226,014
1957	12,423	12,084	20.2	243,942	2,370	2,286	17.5	39,935	10,053	9,798	20.8	204,007
1958	12,343	12,024	23.6	283,897	938	906	23.9	21,669	11,405	11,118	23.6	262,228
1959	13,157	12,219	16.6	203,366	1,217	1,141	17.7	20,192	11,940	11,078	16.5	183,174
1960	12,230	11,900	20.7	246,715	1,673	1,642	20.8	34,141	10,557	10,258	20.7	212,574
1961	12,255	10,852	14.7	159,738	1,781	1,617	13.1	21,185	10,474	9,235	15.0	138,553
1962	10,399	9,965	27.4	272,669	2,418	2,351	29.7	69,732	7,981	7,614	26.7	202,937
1963	11,006	10,637	22.0	233,525	2,047	1,992	25.7	51,247	8,959	8,645	21.1	182,278
1964 1/	11,805	11,455	23.2	265,580	2,398	2,349	28.0	65,718	9,407	9,106	21.9	199,862

1/ Preliminary. 2/ Indicated as of December 1.

Table 24.--Wheat and flour: Average announced subsidy rates per bushel,
February 26, 1965, with comparisons 1/

Period	Wheat			Flour (Wheat equiv.) 2/		
	Gulf No. 1 Hard Winter	East Coast No. 2 Soft Red Winter	West Coast No. 2 Soft White	Gulf	East Coast	West Coast
	Cents	Cents	Cents	Cents	Cents	Cents
July-June average						
1959-60	55.7	55.7	45.9	0	77.3	80.8
1960-61	50.5	50.5	49.0	9	76.4	83.8
1961-62	56.1	56.1	49.9	9	81.7	91.1
1962-63	63.2	63.2	54.5	79.1	85.6	85.6
1963-64	48.7	48.7	42.4	69.4	74.1	75.8
January 1964	64.9	64.9	54.1	80.9	75.3	79.7
January 1965	24.7	24.7	15.1	3/77.0	3/77.3	3/73.0
February 26, 1965	32.0	40.0	27.0	3/89.0	3/91.7	3/91.7

1/ Simple average of daily announced rates. 2/ Flour converted at the following rates: July 1, 1959 to December 31, 1961, 1 cwt. flour from 2.30 bushels of wheat and from January 1, 1962, 2.28 bushels. 3/ Based on domestic market prices for flour which include the 70-cent per bushel domestic marketing certificate.

Table 25 .- Wheat: Supply and distribution, Pacific Northwest, (Oregon, Washington and Northern Idaho), average, 1958-62, annual 1962 and 1963, July-December 1963 and 1964

Item	Average 1958-62	1962	1963 1/	July-December 1963 1/	July-December 1964 1/
	1,000 bu.	1,000 bu.	1,000 bu.	1,000 bu.	1,000 bu.
Supply					
Carryover, July 1					
Stocks on farms	2,695	4,183	1,636	1,636	1,765
Stocks off farms	54,029	22,838	14,840	14,840	10,088
Total	56,724	27,021	16,476	16,476	11,853
Production	103,044	102,883	111,026	111,026	125,843
Inshipments by rail and truck 2/	50,533	58,390	78,311	44,746	29,565
Total supply	210,301	188,294	205,613	172,248	167,261
Disappearance					
Used for seed and feed	5,774	4,995	4,733	3,470	5,650
Milled for flour	37,432	35,392	36,862	16,711	14,560
Total domestic	43,206	40,387	41,595	20,181	20,210
Outshipments by rail and water 3/	118,865	136,673	166,342	82,647	49,730
Total disappearance	162,071	177,060	207,937	102,828	69,940
Carryover, June 30	50,928	16,476	11,853	74,767	98,371
Total distribution	212,999	193,536	219,790	177,595	168,311
Difference, unaccounted 5/	-2,698	-5,242	-13,977	-5,347	-1,050

1/ Preliminary. 2/ Grain, only. Imports included with inshipments. 3/ Grain, only. Water outshipments are inspections for export. 4/ Difference between total supplies and total distribution due to unrecorded truck inshipments and unknown errors in the estimates. Minus sign indicates total distribution exceeds total supply.

Data made available through the Northwest Wheat Project carried on jointly by the Oregon Wheat commission, Washington State Department of Agriculture, and Agricultural Estimates Division, Statistical Reporting Service, USDA.

Table 26.- Wheat: Production in major producing countries and world, average 1955-59, annual 1960-64

Country and continent	Average 1955-59	1960	1961	1962	1963	1964 1/
	Mil. bu.	Mil. bu.	Mil. bu.	Mil. bu.	Mil. bu.	Mil. bu.
United States	1,095	1,357	1,235	1,094	1,142	1,290
Canada	466	518	283	566	723	600
Total North America 2/	1,606	1,925	1,571	1,715	1,927	1,965
France 3/	358	405	352	509	377	500
West Germany 3/	139	182	148	168	178	191
Italy 3/	330	250	305	349	299	316
Spain	165	130	126	177	179	145
United Kingdom	102	112	96	146	112	138
Total Western Europe 2/	1,313	1,325	1,265	1,620	1,367	1,570
Eastern Europe 2/	552	590	600	625	633	645
U.S.S.R.	1,910	1,700	1,900	2,000	1,500	2,000
Turkey	228	260	225	250	290	260
India	330	377	404	442	398	357
Pakistan	133	145	141	149	155	154
Total Asia 2/	1,890	1,920	1,865	1,995	1,965	1,995
Africa	195	210	160	210	235	215
Argentina	226	150	190	190	300	335
Total South America 2/	324	235	265	280	370	425
Australia	168	274	247	307	328	390
Total Oceania 2/	173	283	254	316	338	400
Total World 2/	7,965	8,185	7,880	8,760	8,335	9,215

1/ Preliminary. 2/ Estimated totals, including allowances for any missing data for countries shown and for producing countries not shown. 3/ Major producers in European Common Market

Foreign Agricultural Service, Grain Division

Table 27.--Wheat and flour: U.S. exports by country of destination,
July-December 1963 and July-December 1964 1/

Destination	July-December 1963			July-December 1964		
	Wheat	Flour 2/	Total	Wheat	Flour 2/	Total
	1,000 bushels	1,000 bushels	1,000 bushels	1,000 bushels	1,000 bushels	1,000 bushels
Western Hemisphere:						
Canada 3/	23,231	139	23,370	8,399	118	8,517
Mexico	2	595	597	23	580	603
British Honduras	--	113	113	--	107	107
Canal Zone	--	4	4	--	5	5
Costa Rica	2	393	395	2	390	392
El Salvador	700	55	755	412	45	457
Guatemala	1,092	45	1,137 r	1,005	56	1,061
Honduras	326	61	387	476	55	531
Nicaragua	118	116	234	255	71	326
Panama, Republic of	414	159	573	510	109	619
Bahamas	4/	14	14	--	12	12
Barbados	20	49	69	9	54	63
Dominican Republic	801	71	872	520	94	614
Haiti	808	78	886	883	50	933
Jamaica	6	379	385	--	667	667
Leeward and Windward Islands	--	33	33	--	44	44
Netherlands Antilles	--	147	147	--	169	169
French West Indies	--	--	--	--	2	2
Trinidad and Tobago	2	628	630	4/	560	560
Argentina	--	13	13	--	5	5
Bolivia	--	2,380	2,380	1	3,106	3,107
Brazil	20,626	143	20,769	38,216	429	38,645
British Guiana	--	497	497	11	652	663
Chile	994	356	1,350	5,058	915	5,973
Colombia	2,447	361	2,808	2,571	160	2,731
Ecuador	332	74	406	633	73	706
Paraguay	155	126	281	778	13	791
Peru	2,558	140	2,698	1,249	186	1,435
Surinam	--	164	164	--	209	209
Uruguay	--	21	21	--	20	20
Venezuela	4,762	147	4,909	5,042	126	5,168
Total	59,396	7,501	66,897	66,053	9,082	75,135
Western Europe:						
EEC						
Belgium-Luxembourg	3,076	17	3,093	316	4	320
France	6,550	--	6,550	892	3	895
Italy	3,293	1,416	4,709	2,693	967	3,660
Netherlands	8,552	759	9,311	4,608	510	5,118
West Germany	6,208	8	6,216	998	6	1,004
Total	27,679	2,200	29,879	9,507	1,490	10,997
Other Western Europe:						
Azores	44	--	44	232	--	232
Cyprus	377	11	388	--	4/	4/
Denmark	19	--	19	--	2	2
Finland	--	4/	4/	209	4/	209
Gibraltar	--	3	3	--	5	5
Greece	909	970	1,879	1	463	464
Iceland	6	185	191	6	198	204
Ireland	102	--	102	75	--	75
Malta	--	--	--	--	18	18
Norway	1,338	10	1,348	--	--	--
Portugal	1,234	401	1,635	2,229	579	2,808
Spain	3,352	--	3,352	--	241	241
Sweden	438	6	444	20	4	24
Switzerland	4,385	--	4,385	455	4/	455
Turkey	5,739	161	5,500	4,397	79	4,476
United Kingdom	7,903	103	8,006	938	151	1,089
Total	25,846	1,850	27,696	8,562	1,740	10,302
Eastern Europe:						
Hungary	4,564	--	4,564	--	--	--
Poland	5,552	429	5,981	913	325	1,238
Rumania	--	--	--	41	--	41
Yugoslavia	1,902	748	2,650	13,615	359	13,974
Total	12,018	1,177	13,195	14,569	684	15,253
Total Europe	65,543	5,227	70,770	32,638	3,914	36,552

Continued-

Table 27.- Wheat and flour: U.S. exports by country of destination,
July-December 1963 and July-December 1964 (Continued)

Destination	July-December 1963			July-December 1964		
	Wheat	Flour 2/	Total	Wheat	Flour 2/	Total
	1,000 bushels	1,000 bushels	1,000 bushels	1,000 bushels	1,000 bushels	1,000 bushels
Asia:						
Aden	--	--	--	--	14	14
Afghanistan	1,286	1	1,287	40	1	41
Arabia Peninsula States	110	33	143	--	76	76
Bahrein	--	264	264	--	275	275
Cambodia	--	8	8	--	--	--
Ceylon	--	932	932	--	628	628
India	74,800	105	74,905	121,812	166	121,978
Indonesia	--	447	447	--	10	10
Iran	843	320	1,163	7,183	100	7,283
Iraq	1,847	19	1,866	31	567	598
Israel	4,086	34	4,120	3,902	90	3,992
Jordan	912	2,365	3,277	--	1,721	1,721
Kuwait	11	509	520	24	485	509
Laos	4	57	61	--	34	34
Lebanon	45	704	749	--	680	680
Macao	--	77	77	--	57	57
Malaysia	47	80	127	36	55	91
Pakistan	37,789	26	37,815	36,696	51	36,747
Philippines	5,739	253	5,992	2,676	280	2,956
Saudi Arabia	46	1,649	1,695	121	2,166	2,287
Syrian Arab Republic	--	--	--	--	35	35
Thailand	--	26	26	--	41	41
Vietnam	6	1,172	1,178	111	1,642	1,753
Hong Kong	98	371	469	101	215	316
Japan	35,779	1,419	37,198	25,048	368	25,416
Korea	13,251	553	13,804	8,344	3,052	11,396
Nansei and Nanpo Islands	425	310	735	429	293	722
Taiwan	6,198	646	6,844	6,680	319	6,999
Total	183,322	12,380	195,702	213,234	13,421	226,655
Africa:						
Algeria	5,348	661	6,009	3,176	235	3,411
Libya	--	182	182	--	2	2
Morocco	1,438	1,340	2,778	75	1,682	1,757
Sudan	1,178	1,352	2,530	1,318	1,424	2,742
Tunisia	1,297	88	1,385	382	176	558
United Arab Republic	15,771	13,806	29,577	19,585	17,258	36,843
Angola	456	47	503	471	46	517
Burundi and Rwanda	--	--	--	--	5	5
Cameroon, Federal Republic of	--	33	33	--	37	37
Canary Islands	--	5	5	449	--	449
Congo (Leopoldville)	72	3,203	3,275	63	1,388	1,451
Gabon	--	--	--	--	4	4
Ghana	4	86	90	--	78	78
Guinea	--	--	--	--	1	1
Liberia	3	53	56	1	74	75
Madeira Islands	287	32	319	275	17	292
Mauritania	--	--	--	--	3	3
British East Africa	116	62	178	--	--	--
Nigeria	839	36	875	1,503	11	1,514
Sierra Leone	--	77	77	--	60	60
Senegal	--	--	--	4/	15	15
Togo	239	--	239	--	4	4
Western Africa, n.e.c.	19	34	53	--	11	11
Western Portuguese Africa	--	32	32	--	27	27
Ethiopia	--	20	20	--	14	14
French Somaliland	8	33	41	--	30	30
Kenya	--	--	--	3	6	9
Malagasy Republic	2	9	11	17	10	27
Mozambique	123	4/	123	--	1	1
Somali Republic	1	--	1	--	18	18
South Africa, Republic of	3,045	32	3,077	--	1	1
North Rhodesia, South Rhodesia Nyasaland	52	--	52	438	--	438
Total	30,298	21,223	51,521	27,756	22,638	50,394
Oceania:						
Australia	--	3	3	--	5	5
British West Pacific Islands	--	2	2	--	5	5
New Zealand	--	1	1	--	2	2
Trust Territory of the Pacific	--	21	21	--	37	37
Total	--	27	27	--	49	49
World total	338,559	46,358	384,917	339,681	49,104	388,785

1/ Data includes shipments for relief or charity. 2/ Grain equivalent. 3/ The bulk of exports to Canada are for transhipment to other destination. 4/ Less than 500 bushels.

Foreign Agricultural Service, Grain Division. Compiled from reports of the Bureau of the Census.

Table 28.- Wheat: Supply and disappearance, Canada, France, Australia
and Argentina, average 1955-59, annual 1960-64

Year beginning August 1	Canada				
	Supply			Disappearance	
	Carryover 1/	Production	Total 2/	Domestic 2/	Exports including flour
	Million bushels	Million bushels	Million bushels	Million bushels	Million bushels
Average 1955-59	617.2	465.6	1,082.9	159.3	293.8
1960	599.6	518.4	1,118.0	157.0	353.2
1961	607.8	283.4	891.2	142.2	358.0
1962	391.0	565.6	956.6	138.1	331.3
1963 3/	487.2	723.5	1,210.7	159.0	591.1
1964 3/	460.6	600.4	1,061.0		

Year beginning July 1	France				
Average 1955-59	62.6	358.2	450.4	328.9	59.9
1960	68.7	405.0	492.5	349.2	57.2
1961	86.1	351.8	454.2	325.4	66.8
1962	62.C	509.0	596.1	367.4	109.4
1963 3/	119.3	376.6	524.9	334.8	98.4
1964 3/	91.7	500.4	614.0		

Year beginning December 1	Australia				
Average 1955-59	62.1	168.3	230.4	72.3	102.3
1960	63.7	273.7	337.4	77.7	231.4
1961	28.3	247.2	275.5	79.3	178.0
1962	18.2	306.9	325.1	72.8	228.8
1963 3/	23.5	328.0	351.5	77.6	253.9
1964 3/	20.0	390.0	410.0		

Year beginning December 1	Argentina				
Average 1955-59	68.6	225.7	294.3	139.6	91.7
1960	60.0	150.0	210.0	135.0	40.0
1961	35.0	190.0	225.0	100.6	99.0
1962	25.4	190.0	215.4	123.5	66.0
1963 3/	25.9	300.0	325.9	133.7	126.1
1964 3/	66.1	335.0	401.1		

1/ From previous crops.
2/ Supply and disappearance from Canada and France include imports. Australian and Argentine
imports are generally insignificant.
3/ Preliminary.

Compiled from records of Foreign Agricultural Service.

Table 29.- Capacity of off-farm commercial grain storage facilities,
by States, January 1, 1965, with comparisons 1/

State	Rated off-farm storage capacity on January 1			
	1962	1963	1964	1965
	1,000 bushels	1,000 bushels	1,000 bushels	1,000 bushels
New England	8,160	8,290	7,920	7,710
New York	82,960	75,080	70,680	69,220
New Jersey	6,730	4,610	4,440	4,440
Pennsylvania	23,660	23,660	25,440	26,120
Ohio	130,000	139,000	139,000	141,000
Indiana	122,700	127,600	123,700	126,500
Illinois	405,100	413,900	409,500	414,400
Michigan	46,140	47,920	49,910	48,360
Wisconsin	107,700	107,500	107,800	107,700
Minnesota	307,600	309,700	312,900	309,400
Iowa	362,000	359,800	348,300	351,800
Missouri	185,200	185,300	184,400	182,900
North Dakota	135,500	134,900	136,900	141,000
South Dakota	85,140	85,600	84,610	84,600
Nebraska	494,300	491,300	492,000	491,000
Kansas	836,600	845,500	851,200	849,000
Delaware	5,190	5,610	5,720	5,790
Maryland	19,450	22,260	23,340	23,270
Virginia	15,990	15,910	16,600	17,030
West Virginia	460	450	450	450
North Carolina	23,850	24,050	27,100	27,300
South Carolina	11,640	14,180	15,060	15,390
Georgia	19,300	19,600	19,960	19,000
Florida	2,620	2,230	2,640	2,930
Kentucky	24,200	24,120	24,220	23,340
Tennessee	34,260	35,860	35,870	38,520
Alabama	12,940	11,780	12,500	12,740
Mississippi	23,500	26,500	26,900	27,700
Arkansas	107,000	90,000	98,650	105,450
Louisiana	58,610	54,220	57,250	52,250
Oklahoma	256,100	255,000	240,000	236,000
Texas	915,000	919,000	910,000	905,000
Montana	46,300	47,470	48,040	47,330
Idaho	45,500	44,420	44,470	43,350
Wyoming	5,470	5,690	5,750	6,440
Colorado	76,780	76,780	81,500	81,000
New Mexico	15,870	16,030	16,920	17,630
Arizona	16,770	16,250	16,550	16,780
Utah	14,710	15,190	15,100	16,020
Nevada	2,100	2,120	1,400	1,370
Washington	170,000	160,000	157,200	149,000
Oregon	87,460	87,750	73,760	65,730
California	121,600	119,100	112,500	111,200
United States total	5,472,160	5,471,230	5,438,150	5,423,160

1/ The capacity data, by States, include all elevators, warehouses, terminals, merchant mills,
ships under private control, other storages and oilseed crushers which store grains, flaxseed
or soybeans. Capacity data exclude CCC bins, mothball ships under Government control used to
store grain, warehouses used to store only rice or peanuts, oilseed crushers processing only
cottonseed or peanuts, tobacco warehouses, seed warehouses and storages that handle only dry
beans or dry peas.

Table 30.- Rye: Supply and disappearance, United States, annual 1955-64, July-December and January-June periods 1959-64,

Year beginning July	Supply				Disappearance							
					Domestic						
	Stocks 1/	Produc- tion	Imports	Total	Food 2/	Feed 3/	Seed	Alcohol, spirits	Total	Exports	Total
	Mil. bu.	Mil. bu.	Mil. bu.	Mil. bu.	Mil. bu.	Mil. bu.	Mil. bu.	Mil. bu.	Mil. bu.	Mil. bu.	Mil. bu.
Annual											
1955	16.4	29.1	3.4	48.9	5.0	9.4	6.2	4.6	25.2	7.0	32.2
1956	16.7	21.3	3.4	41.4	4.8	8.7	6.0	4.6	24.1	10.7	34.8
1957	6.6	28.5	3.3	38.4	4.7	10.2	5.9	4.2	25.0	3.5	28.5
1958	9.9	33.2	3.2	46.3	4.5	10.0	5.4	5.3	25.2	8.5	33.7
1959	12.6	23.1	4.2	39.9	4.6	8.5	5.6	5.5	24.2	5.2	29.4
1960	10.5	33.0	2.7	46.2	4.5	9.1	5.7	5.0	24.3	7.7	32.0
1961	14.2	27.5	.7	42.4	4.5	11.5	6.5	4.5	27.0	7.5	34.5
1962	7.9	40.8	.5	49.2	4.7	7.2	6.1	3.7	21.7	20.6	42.3
1963 4/	6.9	29.2	.7	36.8	4.7	6.7	6.4	3.7	21.5	10.0	31.5
1964 5/	5.3	33.5	2.0	40.8	5.0	9.6	6.5	4.0	25.1	7.0	32.1
	1,000 bu.	1,000 bu.	1,000 bu.	1,000 bu.	1,000 bu.	1,000 bu.	1,000 bu.	1,000 bu.	1,000 bu.	1,000 bu.	1,000 bu.
Half years											
1959											
July-Dec.	12,651	23,076	3,757	39,484	2,309	6,483	5,185	2,251	16,228	3,235	19,463
Jan.-June	20,021	---	467	20,486	2,262	1,958	451	3,285	7,956	2,031	9,987
1960											
July-Dec.	10,499	33,052	2,359	45,910	2,301	7,414	5,238	2,254	17,207	2,851	20,058
Jan.-June	25,852	---	319	26,171	2,198	1,695	455	2,736	7,084	4,872	11,956
1961											
July-Dec.	14,215	27,476	720	42,411	2,249	8,744	6,013	2,168	19,174	3,745	22,919
Jan.-June	19,492	---	23	19,515	2,301	2,728	522	2,325	7,876	3,748	11,624
1962											
July-Dec.	7,891	40,803	203	48,897	2,382	3,776	5,578	1,651	13,387	11,834	25,221
Jan.-June	23,676	---	345	24,021	2,278	3,474	485	2,041	8,278	8,818	17,096
1963 4/											
July-Dec.	6,925	29,215	313	36,453	2,393	6,135	5,864	1,550	15,942	5,728	21,670
Jan.-June	14,783	---	336	15,119	2,335	535	509	2,133	5,512	4,315	9,827
1964 4/											
July-Dec.	5,292	33,472	1,080	39,844	2,450	7,820	5,520	1,674	17,464	1,335	18,799
Jan.-June	21,045	---									

1/ Includes stocks in interior mills, elevators and warehouses, stocks on farms, in terminals and stocks owned by CCC and stored in bins or other storages owned or controlled by CCC. 2/ From Bureau of the Census. 3/ Residual item. 4/ Preliminary. Imports and distribution for 1964 are projected.

Table 31.- Rye: Average price per bushel received by farmers, parity price, and price of No. 2 at Minneapolis, 1958-64

Year begin-ning July	July	Aug.	Sept.	Oct.	Nov.	Dec.	Jan.	Feb.	March	April	May	June	Average
	Dol.	Dol.	Dol.	Dol.	Dol.	Dol.	Dol.	Dol.	Dol.	Dol.	Dol.	Dol.	Dol.
					Price received by farmers on 15th of month 1/								
1958	.96	.91	.98	.97	.96	.94	..97	.99	.97	.98	.93	.97	1.02
1959	1.02	1.01	1.02	1.02	1.01	.96	.92	.94	.88	.93	.91	1.06	1.00
1960	.91	.85	.87	.88	.84	.83	.81	.83	.84	.82	.84	.93	.88
1961	.99	.99	1.02	1.04	1.05	1.05	1.02	1.04	1.00	.99	.97	1.14	1.01
1962	.97	.92	.94	.94	.95	.97	.97	.98	.93	.96	.93	1.05	.95
1963	1.03	.98	1.09	1.16	1.18	1.19	1.17	1.14	1.07	1.04	.92	1.19	1.08
1964	1.03	.98	1.03	1.03	1.02	.97	.94	.96					1.03
					Parity price 2/								
1958	1.60	1.60	1.60	1.61	1.62	1.62	1.50	1.50	1.50	1.51	1.51	1.50	
1959	1.50	1.50	1.50	1.49	1.50	1.50	1.49	1.49	1.49	1.50	1.50	1.49	
1960	1.48	1.48	1.48	1.48	1.48	1.48	1.47	1.48	1.48	1.48	1.48	1.47	
1961	1.47	1.47	1.47	1.47	1.47	1.48	1.44	1.45	1.45	1.45	1.45	1.45	
1962	1.45	1.45	1.46	1.46	1.46	1.46	1.42	1.42	1.41	1.42	1.42	1.42	
1963	1.42	1.42	1.42	1.42	1.42	1.41	1.38	1.38	1.38	1.38	1.38	1.38	
1964	1.37	1.38	1.38	1.37	1.38	1.38	1.37	1.38					
					Price of No. 2 at Minneapolis 3/								
1958	1.22	1.16	1.25	1.26	1.23	1.23	1.27	1.29	1.31	1.30	1.25	1.26	1.24
1959	1.24	1.26	1.26	1.26	1.25	1.21	1.21	1.18	1.16	1.16	1.17	1.15	1.24
1960	1.08	1.07	1.11	1.11	1.09	1.09	1.10	1.12	1.15	---	1.13	1.12	1.09
1961	1.22	1.21	1.24	1.30	1.32	1.31	1.31	1.29	1.25	1.25	1.21	1.24	1.25
1962	1.16	1.14	1.17	1.16	1.19	1.23	1.27	1.25	1.23	1.26	1.21	1.22	1.19
1963	1.21	1.22	1.42	1.45	1.44	1.42	1.48	1.38	1.34	1.32	1.29	1.28	1.31
1964	1.19	1.20	1.27	1.25	1.21	1.21	1.18	4/1.17					

1/ State monthly prices are weighted by estimated sales for the month to compute U.S. prices. State crop year averages weighted by estimated sales used to obtain U. S. averages. Prices include an allowance for unredeemed loans at average loan rates. 2/ Modernized parity. 3/ Monthly average of daily prices weighted by carlot sales. Compiled from the Minneapolis Daily Market Record. 4/ Preliminary.

Table 32.- Rye: Stocks, United States, by quarters, 1958-65

Year	January 1					April 1				
	Farm	Terminal market 1/	Interior mill, elevator, and warehouse	Commodity Credit Corporation 2/	Total	Farm	Terminal market 1/	Interior mill, elevator, and warehouse	Commodity Credit Corporation 2/	Total
	1,000 bu.	1,000 bu.	1,000 bu.	1,000 bu.	1,000 bu.	1,000 bu.	1,000 bu.	1,000 bu.	1,000 bu.	1,000 bu.
1958	10,249	4,489	5,375	9	20,122	8,212	2,337	4,948	6	15,503
1959	13,147	4,973	6,259	205	24,584	9,623	3,374	4,948	124	18,069
1960	7,266	7,792	4,673	290	20,021	5,122	4,859	3,641	281	13,903
1961	11,647	3/	13,802	403	25,852	7,465	3/	12,375	399	20,239
1962	7,807	3/	11,547	138	19,492	4,342	3/	10,199	135	14,676
1963	13,700	3/	9,912	64	23,676	7,373	3/	7,800	73	15,246
1964	5,581	3/	9,005	152	14,738	3,437	3/	7,254	115	10,806
1965 4/	11,603	2/	9,373	69	21,045					
	July 1					October 1				
1958	2,573	4,019	2,881	388	9,861	19,315	6,284	7,090	165	32,854
1959	4,362	2,154	5,454	681	12,651	13,224	8,702	6,406	574	28,906
1960	1,865	4,284	3,821	529	10,499	18,148	3/	17,395	403	35,946
1961	4,578	3/	9,513	124	14,215	14,694	3/	15,070	139	29,903
1962	1,908	3/	5,834	149	7,891	20,232	3/	12,889	101	33,222
1963	2,070	3/	4,689	166	6,925	11,205	3/	11,460	247	22,912
1964 4/	1,701	3/	3,474	117	5,292	18,235	2/	11,384	111	29,730

1/ From reports of the Grain Division, Agricultural Marketing Service. 2/ Rye owned by CCC and stored in bins or other storage owned or controlled by CCC. Other rye owned by CCC as well as rye outstanding under loan is included in other positions. 3/ Beginning October 1960, terminal market stocks are included with interior mill, elevator and warehouse stocks. 4/ Preliminary.

Table 33.- Rye: Production in major producing countries and world, average 1955-59 and annual 1960-64

Country and continent	Average 1955-59	1960	1961	1962	1963	1964 1/
	Mil. bu.	Mil. bu.	Mil. bu.	Mil. bu.	Mil. bu.	Mil. bu.
United States	27	33	27	41	29	33
Canada	9	10	7	12	13	12
Total North America 2/	36	43	34	53	42	46
France	18	16	14	14	14	15
West Germany	147	149	99	117	128	142
Total Western Europe 2/	267	267	205	230	225	240
Poland	285	310	328	263	280	277
East Germany	81	78	59	64	62	62
Czechoslovakia	38	35	38	36	35	30
Total Eastern Europe 2/	443	453	450	385	395	390
U.S.S.R.	635	520	600	540	460	500
Turkey	24	24	24	25	34	27
Argentina	32	20	21	7	21	---
Total world 2/	1,440	1,330	1,340	1,245	1,185	1,225

1/ Preliminary. 2/ Estimated totals, including allowances for any missing data for countries shown and for other producing countries not shown.

Foreign Agricultural Service, Grain Division.

Table 34.- Rye: Acreage, yield and production, United States, 1954-65

Year of harvest	Acreage seeded 1/	Acreage harvested	Yield per harvested acre	Production
	1,000 acres	1,000 acres	Bushels	1,000 bushels
1954	4,178	1,795	14.5	25,963
1955	5,133	2,049	14.2	29,089
1956	4,546	1,624	13.1	21,288
1957	4,415	1,718	16.6	28,516
1958	4,390	1,797	18.5	33,182
1959	4,013	1,457	15.8	23,076
1960	4,107	1,684	19.6	33,052
1961	4,163	1,550	17.7	27,476
1962	4,891	1,987	20.5	40,803
1963	4,397	1,594	18.3	29,215
1964 2/	4,627	1,725	19.4	33,472
1965 2/	4,360			

1/ Seeded for all purposes in preceding fall. 2/ Preliminary.

Table 35 .- Rye: CCC-owned stocks, by positions and States,
January 1, 1965

State	Bin sites	Country warehouses	Other warehouses, terminals and sub-terminals	Total
	1,000 bu.	1,000 bu.	1,000 bu.	1,000 bu.
Iowa	---	---	35	35
Kansas	---	25	37	62
Minnesota	---	1	44	45
Nebraska	1	33	100	134
South Dakota	66	3	---	69
Other States 1/	2	10	29	41
Sub-total	69	72	245	386
Areas in transit or trust:				
Evanston	---	---	---	59
Kansas City	---	---	---	19
U. S. total	69	72	245	464

1/ States in which CCC-owned stocks are 15,000 bushels or less.
Agricultural Stabilization and Conservation Service, Inventory Management Division.

Table 36- Rye: Average price per bushel at Minneapolis, and price received
by farmers, United States and principal rye-producing
States, January and February 1965 with comparisons

Date	No. 2 at Minneapolis 1/	Received by farmers				
		Minnesota	North Dakota	South Dakota	Nebraska	United States
	Dol.	Dol.	Dol.	Dol.	Dol.	Dol.
January averages:						
1945-54	1.88	1.64	1.58	1.58	1.51	1.59
1955-59	1.33	1.05	.94	.99	.98	1.05
1960, January	1.21	.94	.83	.89	.90	.92
1961, January	1.10	.84	.74	.79	.75	.81
1962, January	1.31	1.08	.95	1.02	.94	1.02
1963, January	1.27	1.05	.93	.96	.90	.97
1964, January	1.48	1.25	1.15	1.16	1.05	1.17
1964-65						
October	1.25	1.05	.92	1.00	.95	1.03
November	1.21	1.04	.91	.98	.95	1.02
December	1.21	1.01	.88	.96	.95	.97
January	1.18	.99	.88	.96	.96	.94
February	2/1.17	.98	.87	.96	.97	.96

1/ Weighted by carlot sales. 2/ Preliminary.

Table 37.- Wheat: CCC-owned stocks, January 1, 1965, by classes, by States 1/

State	Hard Red: winter	Hard Red: Spring	Soft Red: winter	White	Mixed	Durum	Total
			-- 1,000 bushels --				
Arkansas ....:	963	-	36	-	-	-	999
California ....:	5,138	-	-	191	-	-	5,329
Colorado ....:	1,528	19	-	1	5	-	1,553
Idaho ....:	-	-	-	3	-	-	3
Illinois ....:	12	-	-	-	-	-	12
Iowa ....:	1,456	2,784	-	47	4	-	4,291
Kansas ....:	224,840	1	-	67	143	4	225,055
Louisiana ....:	3,375	-	-	-	3	-	3,378
Maine ....:	-	702	-	-	-	706	1,408
Maryland ....:	601	1,751	11	1	-	2,204	4,568
Massachusetts ....:	-	405	2	-	-	376	783
Minnesota ....:	2,430	59,344	-	2	1	12,134	73,911
Mississippi ....:	239	-	-	-	-	-	239
Missouri ....:	10,799	-	119	2	345	-	11,265
Montana ....:	3,400	4,270	44	1	45	356	8,116
Nebraska ....:	43,137	75	2/	52	22	2/	43,286
New Jersey ....:	-	195	-	-	-	-	195
New Mexico ....:	1,794	-	-	-	-	-	1,794
New York ....:	-	8,661	-	7	-	4,622	13,290
North Dakota ....:	667	53,231	-	-	-	6,500	60,398
Oklahoma ....:	33,953	-	-	-	55	-	34,008
Oregon ....:	2,750	-	-	1	2	-	2,753
Pennsylvania ....:	-	499	56	1	-	-	556
South Dakota ....:	7,824	24,673	3	3	4	54	32,561
Texas ....:	62,116	-	14	-	92	-	62,222
Utah ....:	16	-	-	-	-	-	16
Virginia ....:	-	19	-	-	-	194	213
Washington ....:	6,322	31	2/	4	3	-	6,360
Wisconsin ....:	1,064	6,051	29	-	-	5,672	12,816
Wyoming ....:	-	-	-	88	-	-	88
All other positions:	96,276	3,783	-	-	4	-	100,063
Total ....:	510,700	166,494	314	471	728	32,822	711,529

1/ Bin Sites, country warehouses, terminals, sub-terminals and other positions.
2/ Less than 500 bushels.
ASCS - IMD.

- - - - - - - - - - - - -
I N D E X   O F   T A B L E S
- - - - - - - - - - - -

Index of Statistical Tables in the Wheat Situation, for Calendar Year 1964

WHEAT: Issue
  Acreage, Yield and Production; Control Programs
    United States acreage, yield and production .... February, July
    United States acreage and production, by regions .... July
    World acreage, yield and production .... February, October
    Acreage allotments and program participation .... May, July, October

  CCC: Price Support Operations, Disposition and Stocks
    Price support operations, historical .... July
    Loan activity .... February, May, July
    Sales and disposition by CCC .... All issues
    Stocks, owned by CCC, by classes; by positions and States .... All issues

  Disposition, Farm .... May

  Excess Wheat Stored to Postpone or Avoid Payment of Penalty .... February

  Exports and Imports, Including Flour
    United States:
      Inspections for export, by classes, programs and coastal areas .... All issues
      Inspections for export, by programs and country of destination .... July, October
      Exports and imports, by Census classifications .... October
      Exports, by country of destination .... February, May, July
      Exports under Government programs .... October
      Export transactions to Soviet Bloc, by classes .... February
      Exports to Common Market, by classes .... July
      Subsidy payment rates, by coastal areas .... February, July
    World:
      Exports from principal exporting countries and World .... May, October
      Exports, by country of origin and destination .... February
      Exports, flour only, by country of origin and destination .... July
      Exports to Communist China, by country of origin .... July
    Canada: Exports, by country of destination .... February, October
    France and Argentina: Exports, by country of destination .... October

  Grain Storage Capacity .... May

  Prices
    Futures .... All issues
    Prices, cash, weighted averages .... All issues
    Prices, farm and parity, and at Kansas City .... February
    Prices in 3 exporting countries .... February, May, July
    Prices, support, by classes and grades; premiums and discounts .... May, July
    Prices, export, major ports .... July, October
    Price relationships of wheat and flour .... October
    Price relationships of wheat and feed grains .... October

  Stocks, by Positions, Quarterly .... February, May, July

  Supplies and Stocks in Principal Exporting Countries
    Supplies available for export or carryover .... All issues
    Supplies, January 1 .... May
    Stocks, July 1 .... October

  Supply and Distribution
    Wheat:
      By classes, current year with comparisons .... All issues
      By classes, long-time series .... June 1962
      Condensed table .... All issues
      Detailed table, annual and half years .... February, October
      Pacific Northwest wheat .... February, October
      Eastern Soft wheat .... February
      Canada, annual .... October
    Flour, annual .... May, October

-continued

Index of Statistical Tables in the Wheat Situation, for Calendar Year 1964 -continued

U. S. Department of Agriculture
Washington, D. C. 20250.

OFFICIAL BUSINESS

USDA, Agrl. Research Service
K. M. Decossas
Southern Util. Res. & Devel. Div.
4-9-60 P. O. Box 19687
FNS-18 New Orleans 19, La.

WS-191   The Wheat Situation

```
:                                                    :
:    The Wheat Situation is published in February, :
:  May, July, and October.                          :
:                                                    :
:    The next issue is scheduled for release in     :
:  May.                                              :
:                                                    :
```

Lightning Source UK Ltd.
Milton Keynes UK
UKHW031808150119
335176UK00013BA/1801/P